Praise

'I was thoroughly caugh
when reading this book ι _____ ..., ,_.. ноdding
in agreement on almost every page.'
— **Bill Lark**, founder, Lark Distillery

'There is so much great knowledge and insight here,
and it's written with such wit and passion.'
— **Ross Hastings**, CEO, Clean System Energy

'This book is chock full of practical advice... All in
all, it's an excellent resource.'
— **Stewart Marshall**, aka Mr SaaS, founder,
Marshall Floyd

'*Gin Ventures* speaks to various markets who show
interest in the business of spirits and marks the
possible as probable. If you have the tenacity and
drive, you can.'
— **Amy Odongo**, Marketing and Brand
Manager, Anther Spirits

Dear Alex
Thanks for a great Presentation

Gin
Ventures

A gin **distiller's guide** to starting
your craft spirits business

Happy Reading!

04/07/2023
Bakewell

MARCEL THOMPSON
Foreword by Bill Lark

R^ethink

First published in Great Britain in 2021
by Rethink Press (www.rethinkpress.com)

Image credits

Cover image © Dominik Maier | Adobe Stock
pp62, 63, 72, 76, 79, 80, 81, 82, 122 and 171 graphic design by
Julia Gamble Vale, juliagamblevale@gmail.com
p267 photography by Lauren Orrell,
www.laurenophotography.com.au

This book is dedicated to the next generation of craft spirits producers, those who have made the decision to be bold, to enjoy themselves, to create their narrative and to leave an enduring legacy for all.

Disclaimer

In many countries, you will require a licence to distil alcohol. There are some exceptions; Aotearoa/New Zealand is a case in point. Obtaining a licence to distil and meeting local compliance criteria is now a simple process with the prevalence of online services.

It is important to check the legal status of distillation in your country before embarking on your own distilling journey – and never produce alcohol for sale without a licence. Approach your local distilled spirits association members. They will be supportive of your efforts and want you to succeed.

Contents

Foreword

After thirty years of creating a distillery and help-ing others, I can say that Marcel speaks from a wealth of experience. He has a wonderful way of offering the most useful and inciteful advice to any-one wishing to establish a distillery.

I only wish I'd had this book when I was starting out. Apart from obtaining help in making malt whisky from generous Scottish elders in the early days, I was alone with my wife Lyn in an unfolding distillery business that is today the Lark Distillery. *Gin Ventures* would certainly have become my bible.

I love that Marcel's advice includes seeking assis-tance through membership of craft spirit associa-tions and other industry partners. This speaks to me of an author who is genuine of heart and generous of nature, espousing collaboration and truly wishing you to succeed.

When I first decided to leave the security of a well-paying job and start my own business as a practising land surveyor, I was given some of the best advice of my life. Strangely, it was my bank manager who took me aside and said, 'Try not to listen to people who tell you that you are mad. Those people will probably never own their business. Prepare your plan and follow your heart, and remember, for every bad day you have in business, you will have many more good days.'

Gin Ventures is full of many similar pieces of sage advice, based on Marcel's learned experience. *Gin Ventures* will help you design your plan. *Gin Ventures* will help you carry out your plan.

People come to me at various stages of wishing to establish a distillery and I've always seen my role as one who inspires, encourages and provides guidance to allow those people to make their own decisions. This book will now become my first recommendation to aspiring distillers. When Lyn and I dreamt of making a single malt whisky, we read and re-read as many coffee-table books as we could lay our hands on to familiarise ourselves with distilling terms and basic knowledge. None of those books offered such detailed, informative and practical advice on the many aspects of creating a commercial distillery. As I read through *Gin Ventures*, I would circle and tick paragraphs and statements I found to be well grounded and immensely useful. The book is now literally covered with circles and ticks on almost every page.

For my part, I simply wanted to see if I could make a high-quality single malt whisky in Tasmania. I had no intention of starting a business; in fact, Lyn and I promised each other we would not. Despite saying that and after making many mistakes, we ended up leaving other business interests behind and owning a distillery.

Even if, like us, you initially do not intend to start a distillery business, please do yourself a favour and read this book before anything else. From start to finish, every word, every chapter resonates with our experience over the last twenty-nine years. There are so many pearls of wisdom throughout the book – too many to list. My wish, like Marcel Thompson, is that you achieve the success of your dreams and 'create your narrative'.

Bill Lark
Founder and Brand Ambassador, Lark Distillery

🌐 https://larkdistillery.com

📷 @larkdistillery

📘 www.facebook.com/Larkdistillery

🐦 @LarkDistillery

Introduction

In 1987, as a fresh-faced graduate, I was fortunate to start my career in the spirits industry with United Distillers (New Zealand). I didn't think much about it at the time, but the story behind how that distillery came to be the leading spirits manufacturer and packager in its location is one that encompasses all the questions I asked myself as I embarked upon my journey.

The decision to locate the distillery at 228 Orakei Road was genius. Next to a railway line, with road access, fewer than 5 km from the central business district, adjacent to a natural waterway with space for incoming and outgoing goods, and tiered by natural topography which put gravity to good use. Spot on.

How did United Distillers' business founder Grainger Hannah, located on the other side of the world, visualise some forty years prior what a distillery in New Zealand would resemble? What did it take to do this? To select a location, construct buildings, build a team, mentor, coach and lead people in a foreign country? To ensure that a business ethos forged in Scotland would endure in another country? To produce high-quality product brands safely and consistently, for a relatively unknown market, every day of every week, year after year?

It took tenacity and an unwavering sense of purpose. The drive to demonstrate how business values such as heritage, guardianship and legacy require consistency with community expectations.

After I'd served as assistant distiller from 1987–1992, my career and the joint ventures I was involved in took me to places as vibrant and exciting as Australia, Fiji and Papua New Guinea. I also had in-depth discussions with respected peers in the United States, the United Kingdom and Europe. These partnerships helped me to deeply appreciate what it takes to start and run a successful distillery.

If you are clear about why you want to go into business, what you intend to supply to your customers and how you intend to do it, then that is a promising start. From my experience, most people who start a distillery come from practical 'hands-on' backgrounds. The industry is replete with people from roles in farming and agriculture, turning and fitting, the culinary arts and engineering.

There are always exceptions, of course, such as banker Jesse Kennedy and actor Griffin Blumer who co-founded Poor Toms in Sydney – a case demonstrating that production inexperience is no barrier to success. Pinckney Bend co-founder Tom Anderson came from the printing industry, Great Southern Distilling Co-founder and Australian Distillers Association stalwart Cameron Syme from the legal fraternity, and Dancing Sands founders Sarah and Ben Bonoma cut their teeth in information technology.

Often, the biggest challenge for people with a 'making' background concerns business functions that are not inherently hands on. This book will present newcomers to distillation, whatever industry they're coming from, with skills to solve practical problems and high-level insights into business functions, including approaches to integrating them into a coherent whole: the primary purpose of a business plan. *Gin Ventures* meets these challenges head on using practical systematic advice and language that is easy to understand. Then you can figure when it is time to get expert help.

Starting a distillery is feasible for those who want it; it is within reach. With this book in hand and you at the helm, it is likely to be the most epic call to adventure you will experience.

How this book will help you

Quite simply, *Gin Ventures* describes the steps required to create a spirits business, guiding you from concept to delivery. In Chapter 2, I will walk you through the SPIRIT process, a six-step framework covering scoping, preparation, integration, review, implementation and time. This process will set context and purpose for each leg of the journey, including the use of various models as additional steps and guidance.

Throughout the book, I will include case studies and other business examples drawn from my experience with traditional and contemporary distillers, both locally and internationally. Not all the stories are pretty; there are a few that are more akin to a scene from *Se7en* than *Snow White and the Seven Dwarves*. I include them because the greatest lessons often come from the things that did not work. The dreaded F-word – failure – is as much a part of today as success is a part of tomorrow.

You may have competency in activities that you absolutely love, many of which will be relevant to craft spirits. Unless you can make money, however, your business will resemble a hobby. To help guard against that, the purpose of this book is threefold:

- Part One looks at considerations before you start planning your distillery, like why now is such a good time to enter this industry. In Chapter 1, we find top tips for any new business. Chapter 2 then focuses on a distillery business, while Chapter 3 covers the SPIRIT process.

- Part Two looks closely at your business plan, including fundamentals such as planning with the future in mind, compliance and operations. Business planning – sometimes called business case preparation – is the most demanding and important process to undertake at the start, long before you consider the purchase of land, plant and equipment.

- In Part Three, we will learn about the key cash drivers: product, brand/marketing and distribution. This part will describe how they share important common ground.

Gin Ventures is not a comprehensive replacement for specialist input. Instead, it is a guide, highlighting areas that you will need to give additional thought to on the road to success. It will provide you and your business partners with the clarity, confidence and peace of mind you will need. After all, every adventure needs a clear purpose – and this adventure has the makings of a hero's journey.

How do you start a distillery?

To my surprise, along with a big dose of frustration at how long it took for this lesson to sink in, I have learned over the past thirty years that this question is not the first one to answer. The first question is, 'Who can help me on this adventure?'

Starting a distillery business is not a one-person, one-idea or one-great-product operation. The people involved in the different business functions need to work together, and changes in one function can present risk and unintended consequences if left unattended. Some changes are beneficial, some are not.

You need to think about team structure early and include help from likeminded people who share your vision and energy. You will also need a team of trusted advisors and mentors to save you from yourself. *Gin Ventures* will show you the benefits of going through the 'pain' of delegation and how it will become your business superpower. The best investments you can make upfront are education, broad consultation, planning, regular review, delegation and engaging expert help to assist with implementation.

Be under no illusions, though. As Four Pillars founder Cameron Mackenzie says, 'Starting a distillery is not easy.'[1] Neither is it glamorous, says Molly Troupe of Freeland Spirits on my podcast, *Still Magic*.[2] Cleaning, production, procurement, delivery, equipment maintenance, marketing, branding, social media maintenance, site visits, phone calls, email, order taking, managing complaints and product returns do not happen by themselves. Sleep will likely become a distant memory as you endure sixty- to ninety-hour weeks and your current life will be on hold for a few years if you go at it alone. Over time, however, following the guidelines set out in *Gin Ventures* and with the right people on board, you may come to say, 'Starting a distillery is less difficult than I originally thought.'

The craft spirits journey is an epic adventure chock full of challenges, slaying the odd dragon and staring down your deepest fears, and then returning home victorious. Be bold. Enjoy yourself.

Let's create your craft spirits narrative.

PART ONE

MAKING PLANS

1

Before You Start

'I am going to start a distillery…'

'You are going to do *what*?'

This is the most likely response you will receive when you declare your intentions. The reasons are manifold, but oftentimes the response comes from a position of disbelief or bewilderment, coupled with love and respect. Few people have this ambition; it is a bit leftfield and avant-garde. But then, few people realise that the career decisions they made as an exuberant twenty-something do not need to chain them forever. There is value in resetting priorities and intentions.

This was summarised succinctly by the greatest boxer of all time, Muhammed Ali, when he said: 'A man who views the world the same at fifty as he did at twenty has wasted thirty years of his life.'[3]

Pursue your goals and maintain the courage of your convictions. It will be a hell of a ride, on which you will learn more about business, people and yourself far faster and more effectively than from any desk job or tertiary institution attendance.

Family and friends are often your most likely source of interest in your new venture – once they have gotten over their initial bewilderment. Be certain to have all contributions, pledges and material commitments they make well documented and readily accessible. Note, too, that you will likely work with people across multiple generations, each with its own love language. More on the generations later in the book.

If the monies you receive are loans to you, then be certain to clarify how you intend to repay people. If the monies are a gift, confirm that this is the intent and document the terms you've agreed with the donor so that there is no ambiguity. Sign off on all agreements with witnesses and make sure every interested party has a copy. Believe you me, a little bit of risk management saves a truckload of cleaning muck off fans and repairing vital relationships if things don't quite go as intended.

Why now is a good time

Given that you have probably seen a proliferation of gin and other spirits distilleries springing up lately, you may think that the industry is oversaturated. According to one stalwart of the Australian distilling industry now residing in Seattle, USA, David Vitale (Founder and Director of Melbourne's Starward Distillery), there is room for the industry to grow.

David started the Starward business during the global financial crisis. Some years after his understandably modest beginnings, spirits giant Diageo bought a minority stake in the business via their partnership with Diageo Distill Ventures in 2016.[4]

The craft spirits industry is undergoing a boom unseen since the heady days of seventeenth-century London. The gin category is enjoying such remarkable growth that some people are now referring to this period as a Ginnaissance.[5] However, unlike its inspirational namesake, the European Renaissance, this new awakening is local, national *and* global.

The notion of craft distilling in the UK used to be something of a mystery. Laws prior to 2008 insisted that the minimum size for a still should be 1,800 litres, but anyone in the craft movement today will tell you that is a large still. Then, for reasons that remain unclear, this minimum size limitation disappeared, opening the doors for enthusiasts whose ambition had hitherto

17

been constrained by legislation and capital. The people who helped kick-start the craft spirits activity in the United Kingdom and United States were not from distilling backgrounds, demonstrating that starting a distillery is within reach of anyone, regardless of your career progress to date.

Three different entrepreneurial ventures came to the fore in those heady early days, each demonstrating that whatever you do 'now' is no barrier to future success in craft spirits:

- Chase Distillery in Herefordshire, owned by potato crisp success story Will Chase[6]

- Sipsmith's Sam Galsworthy, a brand ambassador; Fairfax Hall, brand strategist; and award-winning author Jared Brown[7]

- The Sacred, created using vacuum distillation by the progeny of natural science graduate and Wall Street trader Ian Hart, with his partner Hilary Whitney[8]

This flurry of activity was not restricted to the United Kingdom or Europe. Interest across the Atlantic came alive and several disused premises all over the United States became the focal point for creative entrepreneurs to consider their own craft operations. This spirit of endeavour drove the restoration of facilities that had not seen the light of day in decades, Castle and Key in Frankfort, Kentucky, being a case in point.[9]

Hellfire Bluff Distillery in Tasmania provides another great example to consider.[10] Its farm to glass philosophy and sense of provenance epitomises the guardianship inherent in craft spirits enterprises. Moreover, there are great references to how Bill Lark, regarded as the god-father of Australian whisky, took a call from a Scottish distillery offering him assistance when he obtained a whisky production licence.[11] Bill has been paying it forward ever since, helping most – if not all – of Australia's craft spirits enthusiasts to get started on their own journeys.

Now is a great time to start a distillery, but don't take my word for it: create your business plan, taking in advice from mentors, experienced practitioners and your own networks. Craft the plan so that it provides a compelling case to support your ambitions. If anyone asks you why you want to start a distillery, you can then regale them with a great story and show them why it is the best thing for you to do right now. You will present a focused air of confidence to the people you'd love to have on board – and confidence is the single most attractive characteristic you have at your disposal.

What is happening in the spirits world?

At the time of writing, the spirits business is caught up in the economic ripple effects from the trading conditions that COVID-19 responses have forced upon us all, but the state of the economy affects most businesses in most places most of the time. The term pivot has been thrust upon us *ad nauseam*.

On the Sapphire Coast of Australia, the Stony Creek Farm team of Gavin Hughes and Karen Touchie refer to their course corrections in terms of a classic ballet pose where the dancer stands on one leg with one arm extended forwards and the other arm and leg backwards: an 'arabesque'.[12] If you have had to contend with drought impacts, bushfires threatening to wipe you out, flooding, venue closures, hand sanitiser production and a global pandemic thrown in for good measure – all in a twelve-week period – then the 'p-word' doesn't really cut it. Distillers around the world have had to reassess their sales channels, with a focus upon online engagement. We'll delve deeper into the rise of eCommerce in Chapter 11 with a case study from the United States that showcases how important this is for everyone, everywhere.

Trends in low-/no-alcohol products present an interesting legislative and label compliance challenge for governments to tackle. For example, can a producer use the word 'gin' for a juniper-dominant offering that has either no alcohol or less than the legally defined quantity (strength)? This is just one of the manifold examples of an industry moving faster than the legislature.

As a result of the pandemic, the notion of replacing the on-premises social occasion with a stay-at-home event has presented new opportunities for craft spirits makers. The big news, based upon the International Wines and Spirits Record (IWSR), is that gin sales are forecast to grow significantly around the world.[13]

Top tips for starting a business

Let's look at some business basics covering off a typical startup. The fundamentals shared here are equally at home in most businesses and are not limited to producing delicious food or beverage products.

Understand exactly why you want to start a business

Have clear motives. Simon Sinek describes this nicely with his Golden Circle concept and when he says that the purpose of a company is not to make money, but to accomplish something to advance a greater cause, to contribute to society. Money will simply help you get there.[14]

Knowing why you are doing something will help you get through tough times. Muhammed Ali said: 'I hated every minute of training, but I said, 'Don't quit. Suffer now and live the rest of your life as a champion.'[15]

Do not do it on your own

Ask for help. Once the novelty of being a one-man or woman band wears off, you may be too jaded to think about what you can delegate to others. Start thinking about that now for every task in your business.

Get expert help, get shit done. Work out who can help you deliver the things that you cannot do or refuse to do. Consider effective delegation from the outset and throughout your journey. There will be lots of tasks you can ask someone else to do. Someone will love doing the things you would rather not do. Go find them.

Conduct market research – the lifeblood of a marketing plan

Get on to this as if your livelihood depends upon it. At some stage, it will. A high proportion of businesses fail because the need for what they provide does not exist, or there are comparable established offerings already in the market. A unique selling proposition (USP) and adding value is key.

As an example, the drive toward electric vehicles (EVs) is chaotic, with most efforts focusing on the technology and new models popping up with unhindered regularity. If a smartphone is a battery with a screen attached, then an EV is a battery with wheels attached. All a bit same-same in both cases. It is market research, crafting your narrative into your USP and marketing that USP, that will decide who wins.

Invest time and effort to create a well-crafted business plan

A well-thought-out sales and marketing plan is key, so you may need to hire an expert to get it underway.

Look the part

A professional-looking outfit will ensure you receive professional treatment. Invest in a high-impact online look, it is time and money well spent.

Exploit technology

This can help you stand out from competitors, has the potential to save you time and allows you to outsource low-value work to others.

Consider risk in all its forms

Donald Rumsfeld famously referred to unknown unknowns, which successfully confused most people listening.[16] This is where trusted advisors and experienced hands on the tiller can save a lot of heartache when cash is tight, helping you avoid the usual response to an unwanted surprise of this nature: 'Nobody told me about that'.

Expect delays and budget blowouts – and build buffers

Finding cash when you need it in a hurry can be a nightmare that's best avoided as early as possible. People generally have setup costs (capital expenditure [CapEx]) top of mind, but not ongoing running costs (operating expenditure [OpEx]). Every day's or week's delay in production will come at the cost of unsecured sales, so think about ways of preserving cash before inevitable delays strike, and securing cash before you need it. Paying yourself is a balancing act and yet another factor to consider in your business planning and OpEx modelling.

CASE STUDY – THE POOR TOMS STORY

In 2014, an actor, a banker and a business owner walked into a bar. This is no joke, it really happened. Jesse Kennedy and Griffin Blumer were meeting me for a drink and a chat about a craft gin distillery.

Many aspects of that first historic meeting struck me immediately. Here were two men in their mid-twenties in jobs that were demanding, yet unfulfilling. They had good people around them, including business owner Rod Adams, a longstanding business partner of mine and a tremendous wealth of knowledge concerning startups, project delivery and the financial requirements for such endeavours to be successful. A finer, more pragmatic mentor would be difficult to find.

As we sat and chatted, it became clear that Griff and Jesse had energy, enthusiasm, desire, motivation to change their worlds and a willingness to learn. It was also clear what they didn't have, but their determination to bridge the gaps was key. Sometimes when you ask a scary question, you need to be prepared for a scary answer. When I asked, 'What do you have?' I was braced for their response, which came with great pride and smiles that reached from ear to ear.

'We have... loads of ideas. Oh, and a business plan... and this form that we do not know what to do with. Can you help?' With that, a roller-coaster journey got underway.

At the time, Poor Toms had no premises, no licences, no recipes, no raw materials, no kit for research and development, no commercial-scale still – but the guys did have a business plan. As onerous and tiresome as this exercise may be, it is unwise to start any business without one.

PRO TIP

Create your business plan. This will be a recurrent theme throughout the book, so be prepared.

Summary

- Understand exactly why you want to start a distillery. This will help you to create a compelling USP.

- Ensure clarity regarding the monies you receive in support of your venture. Whether it's a loan or a gift, agree all the fine details with the donor, set them out in writing and sign them off in the presence of witnesses.

- The industry looks set to continue thriving, so now is a great time to start a distillery.

- A business plan is key to your success.

- Understand and follow the fundamental steps to starting a business.

- With the future in mind, get in help and start delegating as soon as possible. It will pay dividends in the long term.

- Market research can be the difference between success and failure, so be sure there is a demand for what you're intending to offer.

- Look the part. A professional image will attract professional interest.

2

Starting A Distillery

Now that we have had a high-level look at the fundamentals of starting a business, along with the reasons why it's a great idea to get involved in the distillery industry, it's time to focus more on advice specific to this thriving industry.

Investment in these three activities is essential from the start of your journey, and at every opportunity thereafter:

- Read, listen to, watch and do as much as you can in the craft spirits industry as preparation for your business plans. Social media platforms are awash with information, some of which may even be useful! You will soon learn to determine what is wheat and what is chaff.

- Try as many different craft spirits products as you can as often as you can and document your findings. It's a tough job, but someone's got to do it.

- Devote time to understanding the industry and join craft spirit associations.

Let's now look at the essential top tips I have learned from my distilling family around the world. The first item may be surprising, but all operations need a place to call home, so it's time to consider where that will be, preferably with the future well and truly in mind.

Distillery location

This is a bigger challenge than you may envisage, as securing the right premises is a crucial prerequisite to supporting applications to meet all alcohol-related licencing requirements. To simplify things as much as possible, the options may be divided up into lease or buy in a rural or urban setting.

Take a look at this table giving examples of pros and cons for each option. Then create a similar table for the areas you're considering, and whether to look at buying or renting in those areas, applying objective reasoning for each case.

	Lease	Own
Urban pros	Sometimes more cost effective than buying, leaving you the option to relocate easily	If you're sure you've found the ideal place for your business, real estate in an urban area will generally increase in value
Rural pros	Rents are often cheaper in a rural area	A rural location may be easier to access than an urban one, increasing your options to expand
Urban cons	Rents in some cities are prohibitive, limiting what you will get for your money	As with renting, the price of buying real estate in the city can be out of the reach of many startups
Rural cons	A remote area may have limited options when it comes to renting	A premise in a rural area may prove difficult to sell or make good if you wish to relocate

If you don't have an existing site or property at your disposal that will meet all the requirements of your intended business, leasing tends to be far and away the better option rather than buying. I would recommend you commit to three years with an option for perhaps another three years, but longer-term arrangements can work, too.

Space can be a challenge, and believe me, you will need more space far sooner than you may think. Pallets of empty bottles are one of the biggest bugbears for small operations. Washing, filling, capping and labelling the bottles is the fun part; it's moving and storing awkward pallets safely prior to removal that's the problem.

The craft spirits movement is growing in popularity, fuelled in part by a supportive community that is keen to learn and experience your offering. Events and pop-up bars in off-licence/off-premises locations are now well and truly part of the narrative, so you will need to plan for this and have premises with sufficient safe space to deliver the experience. Of course, attendees will likely want to buy a bottle or two of your offering from you, so be sure to have room to cater for this as well, and be equipped for the unusual occasions when people use cash.

When you're looking for your premises, actual visits to view facilities are a must. There is only so much you can garner from video coverage, interviews and podcasts. In many ways, it's like comparing attending a live concert, theatre performance or sporting event with watching it via your favourite device.

Check out as many distillery cellar doors (there's more on what I mean by 'cellar door' later) as you can and chat to the distiller. The experts are often happy to share their knowledge to further your ambition and alert you to the practicalities that you need to consider. This will provide excellent input into your business plan and help you to build an even more compelling case for people to buy in to your view of the future.

Consider the size of the facility

The first thing to do here is to determine which product or products you intend to produce and in what quantities from the outset. Research facilities of various sizes and organise time to visit them. This will help to drive quality thinking in your business plan and a clear goal around sales and production numbers.

And – as much as I may sound like a busted record – document what you hear and observe. Get yourself a notepad and write down everything, and I mean everything. If reciting into your smartphone's recorder is your style, invest in a yearly subscription with Otter.ai so that you can create transcriptions for your recordings.

Many distillers around the world create alcohol – such as bourbon, whisky or brandy – from a fermentable source like grain or grapes. Rectifiers – which cover most gin makers – re-distil neutral spirit produced by specialists, but locations that distil and/or rectify are all called distilleries. If you intend to be a distiller who produces their own spirit from mash, then you will require a brewhouse operation, and someone to manage it for you. Put operations of this type on your road trip list as well.

The very nature of stills is enough to evoke a sense of romance from the unromantic, wonderment from the unimaginative and awe from the sceptical. They are the product of remarkable craftsmanship and commitment to high quality.

There are several well-known still makers (still fabricators) around the world who have the capacity and capability to meet your business plan's requirements. Interestingly, although lots of people will plan road trips to distilleries, few plan to visit a still fabricator as an initial port of call.

In Australia, we have HHH Distil in Western Australia (WA),[17] Burns Welding and The Aisling Distillery in New South Wales (NSW),[18] and StillSmiths located in Tasmania,[19] arguably Australia's craft distilling spiritual home. To me, this is an opportunity to seize. There are more stills than fabricators out there, so establishing a relationship with one is value-add from the get-go.

Several fabricators have strong online profiles which you can search. They often have key clientele, too, who would likely be delighted to share their experiences with you. You also have the opportunity to establish a longstanding relationship between the fabricator – the spirits expert – and you, the novice. This approach will not only help you, it will also support local fabricators and the craft spirits industry.

When it comes to organising your distillery road trip, spare a thought for the fabricator with a view to visiting them. They are often as unsung as the distillers themselves, but without them, your great art may not progress as intended.

Licencing

Unless you reside in Aotearoa/New Zealand, you will need licences to distil. Yes, that's plural. There is swag of licencing requirements to satisfy in other jurisdictions (see 'Additional Resources' for where to find the requirements for Australia and New Zealand).

Be sure to check what the specific requirements are for your jurisdiction, list them and note them as part of the business plan. This gives the business plan clarity about the requirements, showing that you have sought advice and know what to do. Include plans to find someone to get shit done for your business plan. Reviews and processing times for issuing licences will vary in time between jurisdictions, so factor in timescales, too.

Funding

Distilleries are expensive, so much so that Broken Heart Spirits distiller and founder Joerg Henkenhaf has a simple tip for beginners: 'Bring a shitload of cash.'[20]

Any major purchase, be it a car, a house, land or a commercially viable still, is a significant investment that requires funding in some shape or form. This funding may come from a generous benefactor, family and friends, an angel investor, banks or some other financial institution such as credit union.

No romance without finance

Finance is king. Money makes the world go round; it's a necessary evil. Call it what you may, it's inescapable.

There are two key finance areas to consider: CapEx and OpEx. The difference between the two can be best visualised with the purchase of a car. The vehicle itself is the CapEx part of the equation; insurance, maintenance, wear and tear, roadworthiness testing, energy requirements, on-road assistance, and registration represent the OpEx.

The car is an asset that will depreciate over time. In fact, some wags suggest that a new car will lose around 30% in resale value as soon as you drive it away. Investment in plant and equipment such as stills, filtration systems, water treatment plant, trade waste treatment, bottle fillers, labellers, capping, conveyor belts and so on needs recognition up front as CapEx. Keeping the machinery running is an OpEx consideration, with energy, water, safety and security measures among the considerations.

It can be easy to lose sight of the fact that running distillery equipment is a capital-intensive exercise, which bites hard in the early days of your business, so plan and track your financial outgoings and sources of income up front, preferably with an independent financial expert to help. A practical head unaffected by the emotional investment you are embarking upon is worth its weight in gold, and will likely preserve your scarce funds more effectively.

Cash flow is the most important consideration, in concert with return on investment (ROI) and routes to market. You also need to give due consideration to gross margin and finished goods inventory. If need be, your financial advisor will be able to help clarify these terms for you.

ROI

Expect nothing in the short term – from a financial viewpoint, that is. That's right. Be under no illusions, you are unlikely to be profitable in your first year, unless Lady Luck and a hitherto unseen unicorn combine to bestow boons upon your enterprise. The much more likely outcome will be sixty- to ninety-hour weeks, most likely without a wage

Freeland Spirits Master Distiller Molly Troupe summarises this:

> 'The first tip is realising that distilling is not glamorous… that is the biggest takeaway I can send to any distiller… you are the person who is cleaning the floors, being the janitor and anything… you know, any dirty job that needs to get done… And… if you're not on board with that, then do some soul searching to figure out why.'[21]

Investment in a distillery comprises more than money, though a truckload of cash from somewhere goes a long way. It is time, energy, resourcefulness and an acceptance that the entire journey is replete with different types of problem to solve. There will be delays, frustrations, times when the going gets tough. Expect failures and ideas that do not fly as part and parcel of the deal.

The mindset required to quit smoking, save money, lose weight or get into shape is similar to the one you will need to start your distillery. The ROI in all cases is clear to see. Ultimately, it is a case of mastering the mundane, day in, day out. When you're starting a distillery, the ROI is a culmination of hard-earned small gains, and it's not necessarily financial in nature, at least in the immediate term. The financial returns come later.

But you have a life. What will you do if you are unable to generate sufficient cash to cover bills, family requirements, illness, a mortgage? What will the next three, five, ten years look like? What asset base do you intend to have in place at various stages of the journey?

It should come as no surprise that your business plan will need to cater for all of these considerations.

Funding options

There are various ways to fund your enterprise. For example, Four Pillars, Manly Spirits and Poor Toms in Australia tapped into the crowdfunding route via Pozible,[22] a leading platform for creative projects. This approach first gained traction via craft brewers, BrewDog being the most well-known example in the United Kingdom.

Another significant example from New Zealand is Reefton Distilling Co, best known for producing the Little Biddy Gin range and Wild Rain vodka. This company ran two fund-raising campaigns, the first of which was based solely on its business plan: an outstanding result for a well-considered plan.

When it comes to securing funding for your enterprise, your business plan is more than a box-ticking exercise. Crafted or repurposed in a compelling way, it can be a useful pitching document for willing investors. Time invested in your plan is time well spent.

Planning and scheduling

Scheduling cannot start until your planning is complete. When plans change – and believe me, they will – then, and only then, can rescheduling take place.

One of the longest, most arduous and frustrating journeys you will undertake concerns local councils or authorities and permissions. This is the first activity you will start and will likely be the last one you complete, so consider contingency plans for the inevitable delays that will arise.

The reasons for the delays are oftentimes clerical in nature, such as unanswered questions, contradictory advice, incomplete documents, updated forms that need filling out again, irretrievable documents, internal promotions, case officers on leave, retrenchments or retirements… generally, life happening. During elections, expect the bureaucratic machine to grind to a halt. The sense of uncertainty about the future can cripple the everyday functions of local government, leaving your distillery goals high and dry in the immediate term.

The lead time for a still is also subject to several factors, including design confirmation and delivery.

As a rough rule of thumb, plan for the entire procurement process to take around a year to complete, from paying your deposit to taking possession. The total time will also need to consider customers that are already on a wait list for services, so factor that into the plan.

EXERCISE: Deadlines

If there is one concept that's an acid test for temperament, this is it. If you would like to find out whether you are a deadline rebel, questioner, obliger or upholder, then check out this short quiz from Gretchen Rubin at https://quiz.gretchenrubin.com/four-tendencies-quiz.

It's also an interesting exercise for any team members you on-board.

Throughout your journey, whatever your natural approach to deadlines is may be put to the test by legislators, suppliers and customers, but at least you'll know why this is happening and how to deal with others whose approaches differ from your own.

Long-term plans

You may think it a little odd to look ahead when you've barely gotten the kernel of an idea out into the open, but visualising where you would like yourself and your business to be five or ten years from now is key. Few people expect to remain static, doing what they've always done, in the long term.

Your plans may concern relocation to larger premises, expanding your existing capacity, partnering with likeminded peers or exiting the business altogether. A clear measure of success is the ability for a business to run on its own without you being there, which is an objective worth striving for in a three- to five-year timeframe.

There is another interesting question to pose at the start of a distillery journey: what is your exit plan? From my experience, it is an important consideration, because the long-term future is uncertain. The rate of change a business needs to deal with can result in it restructuring to survive, which in turn has a human cost associated with it.

Missionaries, mercenaries or misfits

CASE STUDY – AN INTERESTING QUESTION

Relocating to Papua New Guinea (PNG) was going to be a major change to the corporate role I had in Australia with United Distillers (now Diageo). Before taking the plunge full-time into 'the land of the unexpected', I had the opportunity to work with joint venture partners there and met many experienced hands along the way.

During a night out, one of the team posed an interesting question to me.

'Are you a missionary, a mercenary or a misfit?'

All eyes swung toward me and a silence fell upon us.

'I don't know how to answer that...' At which point, everyone burst into laughter and toasted my good health.

Once the guffaws had subsided, the team provided me with additional context.

'People have different motivations for coming here, but in short, they can be summarised as missionaries, mercenaries or misfits. It may sound harsh, but trust me, it's accurate.'

And with that, my missionary career as an entrepreneur got off to a flying start.

Consider your own distillery journey. Are you a missionary, looking to build on your heritage and sense of guardianship to create an enduring legacy? Maybe you are a mercenary, wishing to exploit an opportunity to make a handsome financial return in as short a timeframe as possible. Or you could be a misfit, overworked and underappreciated by the corporate treadmill, who needs to find a renewed sense of purpose.

Everyone's motivations are unique. It's fair to say there is likely to be a bit of missionary, mercenary and misfit in us all. The ROI in each case is varied and personal, and it's *not* always about the money. Regardless of how we picture ourselves – missionary, mercenary or misfit – we all have to climb the same mountain. What we plan to do after we have reached the summit – our exit strategy – is the right thing to think about right now.

Sales channels

There are no fewer than seven channels that you need consider, listed here roughly in order of establishment and maintenance difficulty: online, cellar door, wholesale, distributors, retail chains, export and duty free. Let's have a more detailed look at the first two.

Online (eCommerce) is a direct-to-customer (DTC) sales channel. It is the simplest channel to set up with few overheads, other than an online shop, products and content creation. Packaging up goods for despatch is the most time-consuming part of this channel and can erode margin if your offers include free shipping. There are other limitations to consider when you're starting out, such as overseas shipping logistics.

Make sure all shipping and supply limitations are clearly stated on your website. As you grow, you may wish to consider overseas shipping as an option, if doing so makes the expense worthwhile and it is consistent with your business plan intent.

A cellar door refers to customers coming to your location and purchasing your goods there. There are few better ways to engage the public than to make your facility a focal point to attract the curious, enthusiastic, sceptical and everyone else in between. You can expect lots of inquiries from people asking about 'your story': how you got started, where your still came from and how much it cost. Few people will ask about the not-so-sexy things that go into a distillery, such as council approvals, your trade waste management process, effluent, water usage, running costs or the amount of excise you pay to the government, but if you do happen to meet someone whose interest goes beyond the shiny new still and the delicious tasting product, then chances are they have a genuine interest in business.

Branding and marketing

Regardless of the products your team and organisation will supply, and despite your unbridled love for the industry, your business is a sales organisation. To quote Tom Anderson, the founder of Missouri craft distillers Pinckney Bend: 'You don't make money making gin. You make money selling it.'[23]

You must spend a significant amount of time and effort planning how to invest in branding and marketing. Having the best product in the world with no one to buy it denies the gin-loving public a fantastic new taste experience and your own aspirations the chance to make an enduring impression. Market research and analysis is a crucial component of your business plan.

For example, statements such as 'There is a gin boom, get involved' may be true, but they're lacking detail that can influence business decisions. Consider trends and price points in your locality, region, county or state. Join local associations with an interest in craft spirits. Some examples are the Australian Distillers Association,[24] Distilled Spirits Aotearoa,[25] The American Craft Spirits Association[26] and the British Distillers Alliance.[27] These organisations are dedicated to assisting craft spirits makers and have a vast array of resources available. Given that the cost of membership represents a mere fraction of your intended expenditure, this is an absolute must do. No ifs, buts or maybes.

Third-party production

A popular and successful route to production concerns contract packaging. Sometimes referred to as 'cuckoo' in the United Kingdom or 'gypsy' in Australia, this is a legitimate way to get your message and product into the marketplace without the immediate upfront cost of plant and equipment.

In short, you approach a contract distilling company that can provide you with the product services you need. This usually includes a fixed-term research and development route to produce a recipe that best meets your requirements. Other major areas you will need to consider are branding, packaging and label design.

There are significant advantages to this approach, the main one being that you can develop and package a finished product that is ready for sale. This will demonstrate to potential investors, family and friends that the product idea is 'real' and not an ethereal concept without substance. It will also provide cash from operations, albeit modest in size as the ROI on the goods you sell has to take into account the third party's cut.

The usual third-party model has a contract packer producing your offering at the strength agreed upon during the research and development process, packing the liquid up in containers (often 20 litres in volume), and then freighting it to you for bottling and labelling. This is something you can conduct in your kitchen with the help of friends and family, so long as you satisfy compliance requirements to do so.

This process will help you to recraft your business plan as you will now have fact-based financial figures, an overview concerning plant and equipment, and basic knowledge of labelling compliance and bottle selection, as well as operational flows in a factory to use as the basis for starting you own operations. You will see exactly where the gaps are in your business plan, the most obvious being location and the compliance requirements your site will need to satisfy. As awesome as your kitchen may be, it is difficult to consider feeding hungry mouths there in the long term in between packaging runs.

Packaging

The way you present your finished product reflects who you are, where you're from and where you're heading. This is where creativity, operational practicality and financial pragmatism can clash in spectacular fashion.

Packaging for the distiller refers to the combination of container (glass or some other material), container shape, body label, closure mechanism, closure material, back label and neck label. It can extend to packaging for individual bottles as well, the preserve of super-premium plus products in the marketplace.

The source of conflict is easy to see. Your inner financial advisor will be looking to minimise cost to maintain profitability. Your creativity may want to make an impact in branding and marketing, often using concepts that are difficult to operationalise. Practically, you'll likely be keen to make production trouble free and easy, with long runs and few changeovers, and as productive as possible. Few parts and ease of assembly using high-quality materials are key to efficient output.

The product packaging needs to comply with specific requirements such as showing the strength of the drink, defined by national legislation. This will likely need to include health warnings for expectant mothers and reflect the number of standard units of alcohol in the container (a 'standard drink' is defined as 10 g of alcohol per serving).

Gin strengths cover a raft of possibilities, ranging from those best served with tonic to those intended for cocktails such as a Martini, Negroni, Southside or Last Word. In the latter case, the products are significantly stronger than those designed for use with tonic, and as such attract a price premium to address the additional variable production costs involved. In Australia, for example, over 30% of the retail price for a 700 ml (70 cl) bottle of craft spirits is due to excise. Other taxes can bump this figure up over the 50% mark.

Here is the good news. Craft distilleries often produce finished goods in small quantities, meaning that there is potential to command a premium price. This in turn means that the margin accrued from the DTC sales channel can cover the costs of freight with money to spare. Several producers waive freight charges for orders comprising two or more bottles, investing time and energy into delivery approaches that result in the customer receiving a fully intact product, delivered on time every time.

As the product name and producer's story become more well known, shipment quantities will likely escalate to case or pallet loads. This presents a different delivery challenge. Yes, this may be 'in the future', but thinking about it early on is time well spent. Connect with other producers whose journey has advanced further than your own. Chances are they've tackled this issue when their demand scaled up. Everyone goes through the same challenges; the scale and timing may differ, but the problems are consistent. Take heart in the fact that wherever you are in your own journey, there will be someone willing to support your efforts, hence my strong recommendation to join your regional, state or national craft distilling associations.

The DTC sales channel is not limited to online sales via your shop or website. It also includes cellar door, site tour and festival sales, both as finished goods and serving preferences.

Risk management 101

Risk is a term that can fill people with a sense of dread or, interestingly, excitement. All risks and hazards have consequences, which could develop into issues needing attention. These issues may have an adverse or favourable consequence. You need to know what 'a blessing in disguise' may look like.

There are several risks or hazards in any business, and starting a distillery is no different. Risks by their nature are neither static nor finite; they are dynamic and can present themselves at any time. The key is to identify as many of these as you can as early as possible and describe them in simple terms.

One of the best approaches I've come across to support this is the '*If... then*' approach. There may well have been many occasions during your childhood where parents, grandparents and other senior family members used this approach. For example:

- *If* you keep pulling that face and the wind changes direction *then* you will stay like that forever.

- *If* you tell lies *then* your nose will grow.

- *If* you eat bread crusts *then* your hair will grow curly.

- *If* you drink and drive *then* you will be forever branded a fool.

- *If* your distillery does not extract ethanol vapour effectively *then* there is a risk of catastrophic explosion.

- *If* there are no bundings (retaining walls) around your alcohol handling area *then* there is a risk of spillages running into storm water inlets.

- *If* you do not pay your excise liability on time *then* there is a risk of financial sanction.

This table describes five risk-management approaches concerning different approaches to cleaning plant and equipment in your distillery, with examples to consider.

Risk approach	Action required	Example
Elimination	Physically remove the hazard	Use high pressure water instead of chemical cleaners
Substitution	Replace the hazard	Use a less corrosive cleaner for a longer period
Mitigate/control	Isolate the hazard	Clean equipment in a designated area away from people
Process control	Change the ways of working	Engage third-party specialists to conduct cleaning
Personal protective equipment (PPE)	Protect people from the hazard with PPE	Supply masks, gloves and coveralls for people using chemical cleaners

PRO TIP

I strongly recommend that you allow provision and funding for an operational risk assessment in your business plan. Tie this to the location selection exercise as well. If you can, engage an expert – preferably one with experience in distillery design – to assess risk associated with your location choice, but a basic understanding of the terms and concepts in the table will help.

Safety

Safety is one area of your business that is not open to compromise. No ifs, no buts, no maybes – a dedicated and unrelenting approach to safety is essential.

The most obvious threat to safety in a distillery is the risk of explosion. High-strength alcohol could ignite at low temperatures, the ignition sources being as varied as naked flames, welding equipment, sparks emanating from metal striking hard surfaces or static electricity generated by liquids moving quickly through pipework. Treat neutral spirit and high-proof alcohol with respect and choose your equipment sensibly.

Adams Distillery in Perth, Tasmania suffered a fire in February 2021, which caused an estimated $2 million in damage. It was deemed accidental by the Tasmania Fire Service.[28] While disasters can occur in legitimate licenced distilleries, the illegal spirits market is frequently fraught with disaster. In 2011, five men making illicit vodka were killed in an industrial unit in Boston, Lincolnshire, UK.[29]

It is wise to enlist expert help to assess and resolve safety risks that your new distillery may find itself exposed to. There are a series of standards available to reference, such as AS1940-2004,[30] and distillery safety specialists like BECA in Australia[31] or Scott Allen and Associates in the UK[32] that you can call upon.

Experienced practitioners in your area or members of distilling associations are also excellent initial touch-points concerning the safety requirements for your distillery. Reach out – they are there to help keep you and your family, customers and suppliers safe.

And if you still think that safety is a bit meh, check out this excellent article by Angelo Verzoni from the National Fire Protection Association entitled 'Small scale, high proof'.[33] Despite the cute title, the article clearly explains the serious issue of craft distillery safety.

Craft spirits facts

The distilling community is a global phenomenon, made more accessible by information technology, strong collaboration and – in most cases – the prudent use of social media platforms.

You do not need to conquer the world, but if you can dominate in your area, then you can assess if you are ready for the next ambitious leap. Whatever circumstances conspired to bring you to this place, here are some hard numbers to put the industry in perspective.

According to the IWSR, in 2020, beverage alcohol eCommerce grew 42% in the United States – up from 11% in 2019 – reaching $US24 billion in sales.[34] This against the backdrop of a global pandemic, difficult trading conditions, the reduction in international air travel and therefore global trade retail (eg duty-free stores at airports). As impressive as this growth is, however, it's worthwhile taking stock of where you are in the world and assessing industry performance there.

One fact that is not in dispute: super-premium plus branded products are the fastest-growing alcohol beverages worldwide. The IWSR describes these as products in the $AU60, $US30, $NZ75 and £30 and above per bottle price range.[35]

In May 2021, the IWSR released statistics for Australia, describing the 73% growth experienced by Four Pillars Gin, founded in 2013. Four Pillars displaced Hendrick's as the leading premium gin brand in Australia, outpaced only by global behemoths Gordon's, Tanqueray and Bombay Sapphire.[36]

As craft distilleries produce small volumes of well-crafted products, each with a compelling story to tell, more and more customers are willing to pay a premium for this high quality. Success stories such as Four Pillars, Ink, 23rd Street and Melbourne Gin Company bring joy to producers everywhere. Their secret sauce is developing the capacity and capability to produce and sell craft spirits at scale. As a result, 'Drink Better' has become a catch cry throughout Australia.

Options in the industry

The beauty of the spirits industry lies in the multitude of paths you can take. If the big-business end of distilling interests you, the roles are diverse. Any mega company will have production teams to run the brewing and distilling process, people who manage the business, handling marketing, sales, finances, human resources, packaging and distribution, maintenance and so on. Despite being a lot bigger in scale with a lot more people to sell vast quantities of finished goods to, large companies follow the same fundamentals as small or medium-sized enterprises. The big entities of distilling – like Diageo or Suntory – extend past their immediate community, but both options are equally interesting and provide opportunity if you want to work in the industry. It is a matter of determining what's right for you.

For the young and young at heart who are thinking about getting into the industry, there are many opportunities at both local scale and with multinational companies. This might include pursuing a production role using a science background, managing marketing with a professional background, becoming a brand ambassador or sales guru if you have a background in tourism or hospitality, or starting in the industry to learn on-the-job or undertake in-house training.

For those focused upon starting their own distillery, the path is different. Many in Australia or New

Zealand consider the pursuit as a second career or a complete career change. As with joining an established distillery, though, any skills you can bring with you will likely be useful in your new role as distiller or distillery owner. Few careers start out with distilling; most new distillers start out with a career.

There are many training courses available around the world for you to consider (see Additional Resources).

Who's distilling?

People often find themselves in the great adventure that is craft spirits by accident. Think back to your childhood. Did the notion of starting a distillery enter your thinking at that early stage? Chances are it didn't, unless you were influenced by people already in the industry, such as family or friends. There are exceptions, of course, but often there has been a series of events in the lives of today's craft distillers that motivated them to start a distillery.

CASE STUDY – CRAFT SPIRITS DELIVERY IS A HERO'S JOURNEY

Many of my guests on the *Still Magic* podcast[37] exemplify this to a tee. Pinckney Bend founder Tom Anderson has a background in printing; Jamie Baxter came from food manufacturing, such as potato crisps and breakfast cereal; Nick Ayres was a Hollywood movie maker; Kyle Ford was in the military. Jesse

Kennedy came from banking, Cameron Syme from law.

In most cases, they were everyday people doing everyday things, but without feeling particularly fulfilled. Oftentimes, their achievements came at a cost that had steadily increased without them really noticing. Work-life imbalance, a sense that there was more to do, a lack of job satisfaction, feeling undervalued and overwhelmed – that was the status quo. Then one day, something changed.

Many of today's producers heard a clarion call to adventure, to board aircraft to the United States, United Kingdom, Europe and elsewhere. They would return from their adventures, experiencing trials and tribulations in their efforts to fulfil their dreams, confronting their worst fears as cash dried up and delays with legislative compliance bit into their efforts to generate revenue. In Australia, however, Tasmania became a craft distilling magnet, due in no small part to the pioneering efforts of Bill Lark in the 1990s and the willingness of Scotland's finest to help set him up for success.[38]

Let's take a closer look at the people who faced adversity and triumphed. Jamie Baxter was asked to build a food factory for Will Chase in Herefordshire, UK. When Jamie returned from a pre-planned family holiday, he learned that the project was off, but a new project to create potato vodka was most definitely on.[39] Then there's Nick Ayres, a man who was more at home on a movie set until he and his wife Ally decided the future lay in spirits and launched Karu Distillery.[40]

Eddie Brook's family forged their legacy farming macadamia nuts in Byron Bay, NSW, Australia, before taking the plunge into distilling and Brookies was born.[41] Karen Touchie was a government policy worker who embraced her partner Gavin's goal to create award-winning gins in Bega.[42]

Four Pillars is a proudly Australian global success story that started in late 2013. By 2021, it had achieved the accolade of IWSC's Best Global Gin business for the second year running.[43]

But the hero's journey always involves challenges. Following drought in Australia in late 2019, the bushfires arrived. Then floods. Then the pandemic. Venues closed. Sales halted. Supply was disrupted. Supermarket fights became headline news. However, many of our heroes stepped up, producing medical-grade hand sanitiser when supplies were scarce.

Everyday people, just like you, do extraordinary things, every day.

Spirit making and distilling is a mixture of art and science, driven by a relentless sense of curiosity. The nature of these characteristics makes it exciting, relevant and vibrant.

Its vibrancy comes from the growth in interest from people all over the world who share this interest with others. Its excitement comes from the sense of discovery that accompanies every heartfelt desire to produce something that is an extension of oneself with self-actualisation at its core. Its relevance stems from three values that distillers worldwide hold dear, albeit in different guises:

- Heritage – a sense of recognising your past and its influence upon you

- Guardianship – a sense of connection to something important that needs nurturing

- Legacy – a sense of leaving a statement that is yours, and leaving the world in a better place as a result

These values exist in many pursuits, be they artistic, creative, functional or vital in nature. The notion of a distillery that represents a part of you – your ethos, your excitement – is oftentimes a combination of values that is hard to ignore. Like many milestones in life – be it retirement, a sea-change, tree change or life change – sometimes you get a feeling that the time is right. Or it could be as simple as saying, 'I visited a distillery and decided that is what I want to do.'

Summary

- Consider carefully where you want to locate your distillery, exploring the pros and cons of rural or urban settings, renting versus buying.

- Explore all the licencing requirements for your jurisdiction; they vary from place to place.

- How are you going to fund your venture? There is a wealth of options available to you, so make sure you know what they are.

- Plan for the long term right from the start, considering factors such as packaging, marketing and whether you want to involve a third party in production.

- Visualise your ideal business future using a three- to five-year timeframe. Place ensuring that your business will be able to run without you in this timeframe high on the list.

- Safety is paramount. No ifs, buts or maybes. As with many things, more established distillers will likely be happy to offer help as you plan to mitigate the risks inherent in distilling.

- Employ the *'If... then'* technique to explore the risks your business may face.

- Distillers come from a wide variety of backgrounds. What skills could you transfer from your career into your new life as a distiller?

3

The SPIRIT Process

In this context, the SPIRIT acronym refers to business scoping, preparation, integration, review and implementation. All this culminates in your time to shine with the successful launch of a well-packaged and branded product available for supply, targeting your eager customers.

Cash drivers

Cash drivers are the parts of your business which affect cash, both outgoing and incoming. More specifically, their functional focus lies with activities concerning product, brand/marketing and distribution. Each of these have direct impacts upon cash, and therefore business viability.

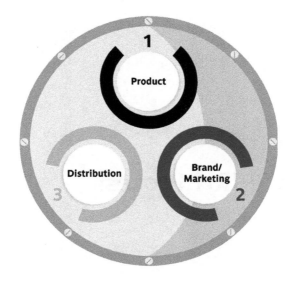

The SPIRIT framework

The SPIRIT process framework will help you to structure a systematic approach to creating your craft distillery. More importantly, although somewhat mundanely, it will identify the areas that need attention in your business plan. Each part of the process describes a set of activities that will apply to all the cash drivers we'll investigate throughout this book.

SPIRIT sets the business context for the three cash drivers: product, brand/marketing and distribution.

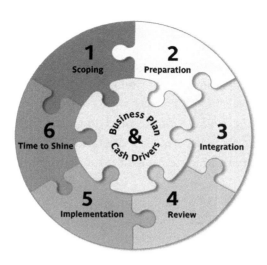

S – Scoping

This describes the 'what': the business-critical items you intend to deliver. As the hero of your craft spirits journey, this requires clarity and selectivity about your intentions and how to put the three cash drivers into play. What do you intend to produce? How do you intend to brand and market your offering? What channels will you use to distribute your product? It also forces you to clarify the things that you will *not* do, ie items that are not in scope and therefore do not warrant focus.

P – Preparation

This describes the thought processes you need to apply to deliver the scope. Your business plan will describe what you intend to do, with whom and how, so each element in it will need considered thought and planning. Some of the planning information for each cash driver may be ambiguous, so this process requires that you consider a way to tackle the ambiguities, plan approaches to resolve them and schedule time to dedicate to this. Resources devoted to planning, problem identification, problem solving and re-planning will become invaluable skillsets in your armoury.

I – Integration

This describes how each of the cash drivers link together. For example:

- You could organise **product** distribution agreements ahead of creation. This is a classic approach of enthusiastic sales folk who secure a commitment to buy, counting it as a sale before payment and without checking that there is a product available to supply. Success – if that is the correct term – will be short-lived at best.

- Tapered bottles are attractive to **market** and help establish an eye-catching brand. They are also notoriously difficult to label, and even harder to integrate into an automated production solution. The collective success of **product** and **branding** comes from mutual agreement and an assessment of the level of risk of each approach.

- Your product's sales folk may delight that single bottles are available for supply to customers, but your **distribution** partner may not agree. Sending out a single bottle attracts additional labour costs to break down a full shipper (carton), retrieve the single bottle, then reseal the shipper and return it to the finished goods inventory. This type of service often needs to carry a premium price which customers may not readily understand.

Approaching the cash drivers in a siloed fashion carries risk as they need to complement each other and all business functions to run as a complete entity. It is wise to use the preparation step to consider how these functions will integrate. The payoff will be easier implementation.

R – Review

This describes pausing to reflect that your plans and reality are aligned. As more information comes to light, you need time to review your current status and check that it is consistent with the business plan outcomes. As the SPIRIT framework provides the substance for each cash driver, it helps to identify areas that need attention and assists you in your efforts to make sure that any changes in one cash driver take the others into account.

Business plans are contemporaneous documents which, at any given moment, may be affected by challenges or changes in prioritisation. A 'set and forget' philosophy will do your business aspirations no favours. Stay alert to new information and the implications this may have on your business plan, particularly if a change impacts your financial viability model and assumptions.

Bear in mind, of course, that the impacts may be adverse, immaterial or favourable to your circumstances. Not all change is adverse, and maintaining a position is not always favourable, but each represents a risk to implementation that may (or may not) require intervention.

I – Implementation

This describes the list of activities and services to support a successful business launch. There are many ways to solve a given problem, but the best approach is a combination of teamwork, time, budgeting, quality and managing acceptable risk. This process needs to consider the preparation, integration and review steps to ensure that implementation may proceed with few issues.

Implementation plans also benefit from having response measures in place in case risks become issues. For example, how will you respond to sales exceeding forecast, safety stock and planned production expectations? The key is to ensure that the response and the intended outcome remain consistent with the business plan's intent.

T – Time to shine

This is what all the fuss is about. The last stage of the SPIRIT process is your time to launch your product upon the adoring public with energy and gusto. By this stage, you will have chosen your product and know how to make it, you'll have your narrative, a clear sense of purpose, branding, marketing and supporting components all in place. You'll also have determined a way to distribute your product that is beneficial to your business and its stakeholders, customers and partners.

The tables coming up illustrate how the stages of the SPIRIT process fit with the cash drivers and their criticality to business plan delivery. Your own table may differ, but this example provides a guide/working example of the structured thinking that will help describe the large chunks of work ahead specific to your business ambitions.

This framework is a useful way to ensure that your business plan takes the three cash drivers into consideration. It illustrates how quality thinking in this context will help keep the business components and requirements aligned.

CASE STUDY – AN EXCITING NEW PRODUCT

The first new product release during my stint in PNG in the 1990s sought to make an impact and meet a market need. This was a classic example of the three cash drivers at work in the context of the SPIRIT process.

The team comprised a small group of specialists with strengths in product commercialisation, materials procurement, sales and marketing, finance and distribution. Branding was simple, distinctive and striking: red and white, which contrasted with a delicious reddish-brown rum.

	Product	Brand/marketing	Distribution
Scope	• What will you make?	• What do you want your product to say about you?	• How will customers receive your product?
Preparation	• The DISTIL process – Decide, Investigate, Sample, Test, Improve, Launch[44]	• Brand strategy • Marketing strategy	• Distribution strategy
Integration	• Product activities that are consistent with branding and distribution	• Brand/marketing activities that are consistent with product and distribution	• Distribution activities that are consistent with product and brand
Review	• Review the business plan • Resolve gaps in the product strategy to maintain consistency with the business plan, brand strategy and distribution strategy	• Review the business plan • Resolve gaps in the brand strategy to maintain consistency with the business plan, the product strategy and distribution strategy	• Review the business plan • Resolve gaps in the distribution strategy to maintain consistency with the business plan, the product strategy and branding/marketing strategy

	Product	Brand/marketing	Distribution
Implementation	• Production plan is set and aligns with sales, marketing and distribution requirements	• Branding and marketing are on song and linked with the product, marketing is consistent and aligns with distribution partner requirements	• Distribution partners are in position to take orders, manage stock requirements, have backorder and return policies in place, and can ship to customers • Stock replenishment processes are in place
Time to shine	• Product is available in quantities to satisfy customer demand	• Branding stands out, is not invisible, insincere or incoherent • Messaging is clear, consistent and on point	• Robust end-to-end ordering and delivery process in place • Clear policies concerning backorders and returns

	Product	Brand/marketing	Distribution
Scope	• A dark rum at a 101 US proof that is delicious and affordable • Made to share	• Bold colours, clear images • Convenient packaging size • Dark inviting spirit colour	• Third parties • Launch a franchisee program • No cellar door • No export
Preparation	• Materials sourcing • Dry good sourcing • Leverage existing plant	• In-house labelling concepts • Engage several suppliers	• Wholesalers • Franchise program for new entrants
Integration	• Test product manufacturing processes • Test production processes (bottle rinsing, filling, capping, labelling, packing, palletising)	• Work with production to ensure look and feel is consistent with brief • Provide sales and marketing materials and merchandise for outlets • Leverage brand ambassador system for word-of-mouth advertising	• Measure up and kit out franchisee outlets • Provide them with sales and marketing support • Confirm pricelists for different tier distributors • Sign off agreements

	Product	Brand/marketing	Distribution
Review	• Sign off on product trials	• Confirm that all supporting materials, launch dates and venues, pre-launch quantities, price lists, sales agreements and trading terms are in place	• Confirm product delivery and marketing collateral delivery dates
Implementation	• Produce initial quantities to support launch efforts on a make-to-order basis • Continue production on a make-to-stock basis and issue safety stock quantities to third-party operations	• On-premises launches • Meet with business partners, confirm final preparations	• Stock is physically available for distribution and sale • New stock-keeping unit numbers/item numbers are searchable • Pricing and invoicing clearly stated, including any applicable taxes
Time to shine	• Product is available in quantities to satisfy customer demand	• Branding stands out, is not invisible, insincere or incoherent. Messaging is clear, consistent and on point	• Able to despatch stock • Replenishment processes, returns, credits and backorder policies in place

Let's now have a look at the SPIRIT process and its links to the cash drivers in the context of your business.

Your SPIRIT process

Scoping

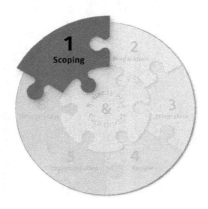

Scope refers to the things that you will deliver and the things you will not. By considering each cash driver in turn, you can make a list of these items.

There are many items to consider concerning the craft spirits product, for example:

- Aged or unaged product?
- Bottle shape and size
- Bottle labels (how many)

- Label design (including mandatories such as standard drinks,[45] pregnancy health warnings, package size, product strength, barcode compliance and scanability)

- Closure types (cork, plastic, roll on, pilfer proof)

- Shipper design (will vary with bottle size and quantity per shipper)

- Bottles per shipper (one, two, three, four, six, twelve, twenty-four?)

- Merchandise (tee-shirts, key rings, jiggers, cocktail books, co-promotional products)

Out of scope may be:

- Canned cocktails, ready-to-drink products

- Low- or no-alcohol products

If you think that branding is something that you'll 'get to when you have the time and money', listen up. Steve Forbes has this piece of advice to set you straight: 'Your brand is the single most important investment you can make in your business.'[46]

Great branding gives you visibility in a place where there are so many competing distractions: 500 m daily tweets, 500 m people on LinkedIn, 1,500 m people on Facebook. Today's context makes this gem from French-American industrial designer Raymond Loewy an important consideration: 'Between two products equal in price, function, and quality, the one with the most attractive exterior will win.'[47]

This relates to all fast-moving consumer goods and includes the super-premium plus category craft spirits occupy. You need to find a way to stand out, and the way you choose needs to resonate with your target. Note this distinction: your target is *not* your market. Your market comprises of both visible and hidden consumers.

Branding scope may include:

- Your company name
- Your values
- Your tagline
- Brand personality and voice
- Communicating your story
- Communicating why consumers should choose you
- Stating clearly who you are
- Attracting your ideal customers
- Articulating who your company is
- Clearly stating your customer promise

- Stating the brand promise

- Brand colours

- Logo

- Fonts

- Distinguishing personal branding from company branding

- First impressions and customer experience (CX)

Out of scope items may be:

- Messages that appeal to youngsters

- Social media commentary or positioning that is inconsistent with your values

Your distribution scope is important. Having a high-quality well-branded product without an effective means to deliver it in full on time to customers is a challenging place to be.

Distribution items in scope may include:

- Online sales

- Hand selling

- Price incentives

- Merchandise supply

- Social media campaigns

- Distributors and agreements

- Brand representatives and ambassadors

- Influencers

- On-premises and off-premises events

Out of scope items may include:

- Retail chains

- International customers

- Export

- Duty free

Preparation

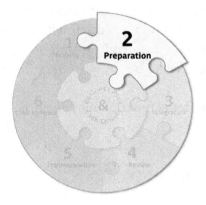

Preparation and planning are concepts that can fill people with a raft of emotions, ranging from impatience to dread and apprehension, anticipation and excitement to indifference and boredom. The focus of your attention needs to be on the start, but with the end in mind. Here's why.

Endeavours fail at the start. It merely takes time for the unseen symptoms of failure to appear as issues later. Plan to engage expert help before, during and after your intended business launch. Identifying the resources that you need is a crucial component in the business plan.

Here's an everyday example to consider. Planting a garden in a haphazard fashion without a planned approach may – or may not – lead to a great outcome. Why take the chance, though, when there's the likelihood you'll end up with weeds and poor produce? The time, effort and resources you'll require to correct the problem later will be far greater than those needed for planning to avoid known risks from the get-go.

An effective planning process is at the heart of every successful endeavour. Workshopping your business plan with experts will help crystallise its intended outcomes in a measured, disciplined and focused manner. Recognise and accept that changes are inevitable, so a set of tools or a process to help you re-plan activities in response to change is as important as the plan itself. Sure, flying by the seat of your pants is exciting and thrilling. It is also exhausting, expensive and short-lived. The choice is yours, and only you can come up with the best answer; one that is consistent with the business plan.

A bit of prior planning mitigates the risk of poor performance and the inevitable fan cleaning that can result. Treat each of the cash drivers with the love and attention it demands, dedicating focused preparation sessions for each one. These will create a baseline plan for reference, which – in similar fashion to business plan reviews – will likely be subject to adjustment as new information or risks become apparent.

Scheduling is another discipline that comes under the preparation heading. It's allied to planning but is distinctly different. Plans describe what you will (and will not) do, and who will deliver that. A schedule takes all the key planning outputs and organises them in a sequence within a timeframe. With the planned pieces scheduled, an activity in one of the cash drivers will likely – though not always – have implications for the others. For example, you cannot distribute before products are available; you can take backorders which will undergo fulfilment later.

Planning and scheduling make up the premise behind several successful crowdfunding campaigns for new enterprises. Products cannot leave your premises in a saleable fashion unless it is legally permissible for them to do so and they are correctly filled, labelled, packed and ready for despatch, be that direct to consumers or via third parties. Label design finalisation cannot take place until all branding conversations and legal compliance matters have been dealt with.

Delays to delivering parts of the cash driver plans can affect the final launch date. Such delays are called critical path activities. Plan to give them your attention and focus immediately.

Integration

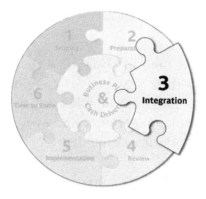

Integration means many things in business, but one of the best definitions is available in the *Project Management Body of Knowledge (PMBOK)*.[48] The results of cash driver preparation are like jigsaw pieces that need assembly into a coherent whole. Integration combines and aligns these pieces to resemble the picture illustrated by the business plan. Like any jigsaw puzzle worth doing, it is a difficult challenge without a comprehensive business plan to reference.

Review

Now is a good time to check how the various cash drivers and their respective components work together. This is merely a rehearsal to ensure that processes, people, paperwork and everything else in between are working as intended.

If any of the cash driver processes are not working to plan, this is generally a sign of a missing asset. The asset could be people, materials, machinery, a message, an email, a communication to the team, satisfying a legislative requirement or a process definition that somehow slipped under the radar. Once you have identified it, address that gap, create the asset and retest your integrated approach with the asset in place, all the while making sure that your responses and courses of action are consistent with the business plan.

Implementation

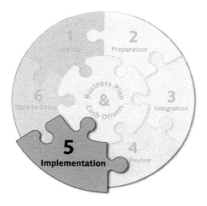

Now you're satisfied that all of the cash drivers are working in concert, ie there are no missing assets, the products bear the agreed compliant label designs, the production plan will result in your team safely producing completed high-quality finished goods in the correct quantities, you have your distribution channels in place, you can invoice for goods and receive your cash, then surely you're ready to roll. Aren't you?

Not quite. The government expects its cut. You will need to satisfy all the documentation requirements for customs and excise. This includes the movement of goods from your facility to a third party.

Cash drivers and government sorted out? Excellent. You can now grind your way to a start. That's right.

This is merely the start of an endeavour that will take you on a hero's journey.

Time to shine

Congratulations! Your product is now available to order and purchase, and all of your hard work has come to fruition.

People understand what prices you will charge, your payment terms and your delivery costs. You understand the difference between publicity and advertising, and have measures in place to maintain sales momentum in the launch after-glow. Your sales and marketing campaigns are working for your selected channels. This in turn will drive the operation plan to produce more stock and satisfy sales demand. You have a good handle on customer service levels and can supply as intended.

Business plan revisions

Change happens. Be prepared. Stay focused.

Projects of significant scale and duration are often subject to change. The sources of the change may vary and impact in different ways. Political, environmental, social and technological changes are often obvious, but there can be legal and economic changes as well which influence the reason for creating the business plan in the first instance.

For example, changes in government may lead to changes in excise treatment, the cost of goods sold and your venture's profitability. Environmental policy amendments relevant to your location may require changes in waste treatment and water usage (distilling operations use a lot of water, so closed-loop recycling is worth considering). Other environmental changes – as varied as drought, bushfire, flood, snow and pandemic – can prompt a rethink.

Social changes such as operating hours for on-premises venues may have impacts, examples being the lockout laws that befell Sydney's on-premises trade in 2016[49] and the law changes that impacted on-premises venues throughout the United States during 2020.[50] Another example is the movement toward triple bottom-line reporting. Where most businesses have historically focused on profit, there is now a drive toward considering people and the planet in business performance terms.[51]

Given the lead time that still fabrication can occupy during construction, changes to operating standards and ratings (eg IECEx in Australia,[52] explosion proofing, intrinsic safety, voltage rating and power supply requirements) may prompt changes to engineering design. Revisions of this nature to original design are often referred to as 'in scope unforeseen' and attract a variation in cost – calculated by the fabricator – that will need your approval before implementation. This in turn will likely change the lead time and delivery date for kit as there will be knock-on effects for work in progress the fabricator has scheduled for other customers. There are a limited number of people available to do the work for each customer.

Risks are ever present, which is why the business plan needs to be top of mind throughout your distilling journey. It makes sense to effect changes to the business plan, then engage other parties to stress test your thinking by providing additional viewpoints. It can be difficult to remain objective about something near and dear to you, but bear in mind that exposure to different types of risk may impact the business plan.

Summary

- The SPIRIT process – Scoping, Preparation, Integration, Review, Implementation and Time to shine – illustrates the steps you need to consider for each of the three cash drivers.

- The three cash drivers are product, brand/marketing and distribution.

- Scope is what you will do concerning the cash drivers.

- Preparation covers who you need on board, and where and when you will deliver the scope.

- Integration is fitting the cash driver jigsaw pieces together.

- Review – making sure the cash driver pieces work together as intended.

- Implementation is the pieces fitting snuggly; the picture is a masterpiece.

- Your time to shine is when your picture is on show to the paying public.

- Applying the SPIRIT process framework to each of the cash drivers will bring the content of your business plan to fruition.

- Your job is to deliver the business plan. This is difficult to do on your own, so get expert help and consider making these experts your business partners.

Suffice to say, this is a simplified and optimistic view of the future, but it's one that is within reach.

PART TWO

BUSINESS PLAN

4

Business Plan Considerations

That's right, folks, there is no way around it: you need a business plan on paper, written in language that is easy to understand. Not one in your head, nor one abstractly formed by your imagination, struggling to get out; and not one of 'those' plans scribbled on a piece of paper after an alcohol-fuelled deep-and-meaningful conversation, although in fairness, this is not an unusual way for a business plan to start. The major difference between success and failure lies with what you choose to do with the scribbles in the cold light of day with a belting hangover.

As an absolute minimum, your business plan needs to consider your motivation and purpose. Neither making a profit nor being your own boss is a sufficiently compelling reason to start a business. A middle-management position in a well-run company can deliver both to you if that's what you desire. Your reason for starting your business needs to be strong enough to get you through the hard times – and there will be many – and compelling enough to persuade others to come on board. You will know when your motivation fits these criteria *and* resonates with you, and that is what will form the basis of your USP and your all-important business plan.

Once you have your motivation, you're ready to consider the substance of your plan.

Planning with the future in mind

An important consideration that often gets overlooked is to understand how you intend to exit the business. This may sound like a curious thing to consider before you have started, but when you think about it, it's not. If you are investing in a house, for example, chances are you will have some views about the property's future beyond the here and now. Maybe you intend it as an investment or stepping stone to something else. Perhaps you will raise a family there and have no intention of moving anytime soon. You may be down-sizing/smart sizing, or it is a vehicle to create equity upon sale.

Everyone's circumstances are different, but often-times, people engaged in a house purchase have clear views about what will happen after the purchase and what they intend to do within three to five years. Treat your business decision to start a distillery the same way. Perhaps world domination is your driver, and this business is merely a stepping stone to a larger version of what you already have, or perhaps it will continue to be all you ever wanted.

Whatever your motivations, there must be an enduring sense of purpose behind them. Interested parties often find this attractive, and it may persuade them to seek inclusion. When this happens, a clear business plan, coupled with purpose and structured with business roles, is essential. Not only for today – it helps map the future.

Ultimately, the ideal position to be in is one where you can get the business up and running and delegate low-value tasks to others so you can focus on your great art, all the while thinking about what a potential exit may resemble. People often underestimate or don't fully understand how hard starting and running any business can be, nor what a realistic financial return will be. The worst position to find yourself in is one where you've created something that is no more than a job, but with a truckload of stress and anxiety associated with it as your capacity to solve problems goes into overdrive.

It is important to have absolute clarity about why you are doing what you do. This assists speedy decision making and helps preserve key resources: time, money and people. Creating a 'no list' – a clear, comprehensive living list of things that do not align with your business plan – is a great way to keep on task and dismiss distractions that would otherwise consume your precious resources.

It is always a wise investment in time to consider the future for your business, its shareholders/partners and the people within it who do extraordinary things every day.

Don't forget the finances

As an absolute minimum, your business will need to demonstrate sound financial discipline and account for every transaction it makes concerning people, processes, procedures, policies and tools. If finance is not your strong suit – and believe me, few makers are naturally good with numbers – then the time to think about your financial viability and a rosy future is now, at the start.

Another reason why this is so important to get right from the beginning concerns financial borrowing capacity. Most lending institutions need at least two years' worth of financial reports (balance sheet, profit and loss, cash flow) showing your business viability to give them confidence that you pose little risk to them getting their money back. Being able to access funds for the next stage of growth is a great position to be in, so plan for this right from the beginning.

PRO TIP

Get a financial expert on to your team as soon as is practicable, preferably at the start. This is an invaluable partnership for your business plan preparations and beyond.

A financial expert will provide continual clarity, certainty and peace of mind. They may also introduce some tough conversations, perhaps questioning your ambitions or at least the way you think you can bring them to fruition. You will then know whether your plans are feasible or not.

Get expert help. That is all.

Location revisited

We touched on choosing the location of your business in Part One, so let's expand on that here. Prepare for a long, protracted, frustrating and stressful 'adventure'.

Whether your business premises will be in a rural or urban setting, leased or owned, somewhere you already have access to or a place you're yet to find, there is a series of fundamental considerations:

- Start with finding a **town planning consultant** or equivalent. Contact local council authorities, making them aware up front of your intent to start a distillery as soon as is practicable. This is time well spent and can help you work through that no list.

- Distilleries have specific **business zoning requirements**. In fact, all alcohol businesses have requirements to meet, so find out what they are. For instance, you may find a jurisdiction where it is possible to operate in an industrial zone without council approval if your planned output is less than some arbitrary local limit (eg less than 4,500 litres per year). Note that if even the location you choose doesn't meet requirements, it provides you with a good lesson to apply when pursuing a different location.

- **Proximity** to schools, churches, green-wedge zones, built-up areas and existing alcohol businesses may influence local authorities' assessments. Make note of these and build a case that considers existing infrastructure.

- There are often **land taxes**, rates or other taxation components attached to a location or building (ask anyone who has played Monopoly). Make sure the business plan assumptions take this into account.

- If you're considering **leasing**, property owners may have specific views about modifying location interiors, exteriors, fittings, electricity or other energy requirements, or trade waste. The term 'make good', ie how the tenant should leave the property at the end of the lease, may be a consideration worth planning for right from the start.

- Distilleries use a lot of **energy and water**. They also produce co-products which will require a form of waste treatment. You location needs to take all this into account.

- Lease, building and pest **inspections** are funds well spent up front to ensure that your chosen location is not a safety hazard. This will give you an indication of any shortcomings that may require investment on your part to bring the facility up to a safe functional standard.

- **Parking** for visitors and sufficient access to receive inward goods and release deliveries are important considerations. This is often tied to the available approved space for patronage in the facility and will likely have a cap (maximum limit). As many operators are acutely aware, a pandemic or some other unforeseen risk can impact the need for this measure overnight.

- Is the location subject to **temperature extremes** that will impact your operational capability? Cold winters and scorching summers are superb conditions for products aged in charred barrels, but not so good for bottling spirits day in, day out.

- **Security** is key. Distilleries are attractive places for villains to explore and plunder, so are there any weak points they could exploit? It is always a good idea to engage an expert to assess a location and provide an estimate for security that will meet your needs and satisfy legislative requirements for a distillery. This extends to bonded warehouses, rickhouses and other locations where packaged or unpackaged goods may reside.

- **Fire protection** and protection against explosion – this is a case of expecting the best but planning for the worst. Jamie Baxter, the Artisan Distiller, describes on my podcast the time and effort he spent building relationships with fire authorities and the police to support the creation of the City of London Distillery in London's business district.[53] It was time well spent and crucial for project success. Items to consider will likely include sprinklers, fire alarms, smoke alarms, heat sensors, sirens and upgraded energy supplies. The City of London Distillery needed a bomb proof/explosion proof enclosure made of glass to contain any explosive misadventure.

- Be clear on how much **space** you think you will need at startup and during business growth, and ultimately a view of the production tipping point which will prompt relocation. Think about buying a house again: every relocation attracts cost. In most cases for a distillery business, you'll likely need to start the location selection process all over again, as if you were starting your business afresh.

Lease or buy?

This question requires context before you craft a definitive answer. The first outlay to consider is location. If you own a location that you can modify, zoning compliance permitting, then you can easily draw this matter to a conclusion.

Leasing a property before you are ready to start operations is a sure-fire way to drain cash. There are a lot of different ways to find and fund premises for your business in a correctly zoned commercial location. To determine what the requirements are for your distillery, meet with your new best friend at your local council, and you'll be able to preserve cash. An imaginative commercial property negotiator is worth their weight in gold, too.

It may be possible to take up a long-term lease (say five years) with an option to renew for another five years. Hopefully, you can find a receptive landlord who is OK with you setting up something like the proposal outlined in the table, and may even end up being a commercial property partner who can help you deliver your business plan.

Year	Year 1 Half 1	Year 1 Half 2	Year 2	Year 3	Year 4	Year 5
Rent	Free	50%	75%	100%	100%	100%

Several people consider purchasing a property as a sound way to get started. Designing a location to your specifications is also an option. Some operators in the agricultural sector have successfully converted parts of their existing property into a craft distillery location. However, for people in urban or built-up areas, purchasing a building or location may prove challenging in terms of cost and availability.

PRO TIP

Regardless of the location, urban or rural, choose somewhere that can accommodate the design you have in mind for your distillery. This translates to a minimum of 250 m^2–300 m^2 in floor space to give you room to move and provide capacity for expansion plans. These plans may require acceleration far sooner than you expect.

Compact spaces can undergo professional design input that optimises their use for operations. A new house, for example, is the product of design input and regulatory compliance.

The location keys to consider are reliable power supply and access points, reliable water supply, capacity for trade waste management, good workflow, good lighting, good ventilation (there are requirements and standards to meet), room for dry goods such as bottles, caps, labels and shippers, and ease of access to store finished goods and shift goods out of the premises to support deliveries.

Plant and equipment selection

The still

It is always the still that commands the most attention whenever there are decisions to be made concerning plant and equipment for a distillery, which makes sense. Suffice to say, the still is important. Equally important are the supporting pieces of plant and equipment. Before you can decide on any of that, though, your business plan needs to state quantities of finished goods you intend to make for sale.

Before I provide a basic list of kit that you may need – bearing in mind that if you intend to age your products in barrels, this needs attention as well – a word of advice. Select the largest capacity, highest quality still you can afford to buy right now that will meet your operational and sales ambitions over a one- to three-year period. Review this position no later than the end of the first year, and continue to review annually.

Why? Because at some point – often far sooner than you may expect – you will find that you do not have sufficient capacity to meet the demands of the ever-hungry sales machine that is punching out your product range as if there were no tomorrow. In the absence of sales, that is exactly what tomorrow will resemble for your business.

CASE STUDY – GET THE BEST YOU CAN AFFORD

During one of my *Still Magic* podcast episodes, I spoke with Four Pillars Gin founder, master distiller and 1996 Australian Olympian Cameron Mackenzie.[54] We chatted about a variety of concepts, including a few tips for starting a craft spirits business. One of his tips was to buy the best still you can find and afford.

Simple.

During an investigative trip to the United States' west coast, the standout for Cameron was the superb gin quality produced using Carl stills.[55] He was convinced that this was the still his business needed.

Carl stills are high quality and in demand, and consequently a costly investment, but the upfront cost more than pays for itself as they produce delicious spirits for people to enjoy time and time again.

Four Pillars engaged Carl's own distiller to mentor Cameron on site in Melbourne. The company then engaged branding experts and a well-credentialed distributor. This meant it was well positioned to address the three cash drivers: product, branding/ marketing and distribution. Each one of these drivers is difficult to tackle. Individually, they stretch the capacity and capability of a single person trying to do it all, likely leading to suboptimal outcomes.

The Four Pillars success story demonstrates that it pays to get the best you can afford, particularly when considering something as essential as the still.

CASE STUDY – STILLSMITHS, THE FABRICATORS' VIEW

Mark Kolodziej and Tim Freeman are co-founders of StillSmiths, a still design, fabrication and distillery business located in Westbury, Tasmania – Australia's very own Apple Isle.[56] Their business kicked off in 2017 in response to market demand for high-quality stills, driven by a surge in interest from would-be distillers in Tasmania. It was a case of intrepid creators looking to make their mark in the industry's spiritual home and needing help to bring this to fruition.

Mark's tips for new entrants into the craft spirits industry are clear and easy to understand:

- Work out how much you intend to make annually.
- Work out how many days you intend to work annually to make this quantity.
- Work out what size still you need to run on the days required to meet that planned output.

In other words, your business plan needs to start with the end in mind, and then work out who, what, where and when. For instance, if you want to make 10,000 x 700 ml bottles at 40% for sale each year, at the rate of 100 bottles per day, that's 100 days of production, roughly three days per week for thirty-three weeks of the year. Once you know all this, then you can think about the still capacity. Bear in mind, of course, you'll likely want to be in business for more than a year, so your choice needs to consider forecasts in sales growth in subsequent years.

Mark and Tim's company makes a range of wonderful stills from 300 litres to 11,500 litres. Customers include domestic producers such as Lark Distillery and international producers such as Reefton Distilling Co. in Aotearoa/New Zealand.

With Tasmania producing world-class award-winning products year in, year out, unsurprisingly, StillSmiths' immediate ambitions include becoming the best still manufacturer in the southern hemisphere. Given the energy, desire and sense of purpose Mark and Tim possess by the barrel load, it is merely a matter of when, not if.

You may find a company close to your neck of the woods that can supply kit to meet your requirements, all based on your business plan. For example, Genio Stills, based in Poland, has agency in the United Kingdom.[57] In the United States, there is Vendome Copper Brass works.[58] In Australia, there's HHH Distil in WA,[59] Burns Welding in NSW[60] and Still-Smiths in Tasmania,[61] all providing superb products and services.

Whomever you choose, it's a wise investment of time and energy to build working relationships with still fabricators. The stills last a lifetime and are the result of lots of love and attention, sometimes spanning several generations. Make the time for the fabricator early, and the fabricator will make the time for you.

Once you have sat down, recovered from the decision to send a 50% deposit to a still manufacturer and allowed the shock to subside, think about other equipment to purchase.

Other equipment you will need

Water. Lots of it. You will need water for use around the plant, spirit reduction and still charges. Distilleries use a lot of water, so explore options to conserve and reuse it as part of your plant design. This plays into requirements for effluent treatment and disposal as well. You will also need to consider trade waste disposal.

In addition to a good water supply, you will need strength testing and volumetric measuring equipment. Take a two-stage approach:

- Calibrated hydrometers and thermometers.

- Provision for a handheld electronic strength testing device such as an Anton-Paar density meter.[62] These are expensive value-add items in the immediate term, but a worthwhile investment in the long term.

This will then make the hydrometers and thermometers an excellent backup solution in the unlikely event that the density meter fails.

Power supply – check what your requirements are. Chances are that you'll need three-phase and several single-phase power outlets, plus an upgraded power box to meet the electrical energy requirements to run the plant and equipment.

Also consider:

- Leasing a forklift or hand trolley to move palletised items or barrels.

- A bonded area in the location to store finished goods.

- Barrels if you are planning to make rum, whisky, brandy or other products that require wood ageing – this decision will play into the location size that you have in mind, so choose carefully and plan for future growth now.

- Fireproof pumps and food-grade pipework to move spirits and water around the location.

- Botanical storage – dry temperature-controlled room.

- Dry goods storage for bottles. These are generally delivered in pallet lots and are a menace to store and move. You may be able to use the pallets to store packaged finished goods once the bottles are filled, but they are still a storage challenge that needs some thought and attention.

- Receiving dock/receiving space – you will need room to take delivery of dry goods, spirits, plant and equipment. The location flow of materials is also a key consideration.

- Bottle labelling – it's likely that you will have to apply approved labels by hand. There are several different manual label applicators available, so choose wisely so that they can handle your labels.

- Prominent signage – sometimes, the fewer people who know what you're up to, the better. Alcohol and raw materials are an inviting mix for a villainous mind, so beware. Make sure – as unlikely as this sounds – that the still and other plant and equipment cannot undergo forcible removal.

- Stainless steel tanks – you will need these for the reduction processes to bring your hard-earned spirits production to bottling strength. Make sure they are easily accessible for cleaning and have functioning outlets that do not leak with access to drainage as appropriate.

- Water treatment equipment – a reverse osmosis kit provides an effective low-cost solution at the start.

- Stainless steel buckets.

- A paddle for mixing.

- A way to measure volume. Wooden dipsticks work well.

- Four head volumetric filling machine.

This does not need to happen all at once; it is a little like buying furniture for a house bit by bit.

Business structure

This is one of 'those' things that may experience a light touch in the preparation of a business plan, but oftentimes gets put on the back burner. Most excise collection agencies need confidence that you will pay your excise to them, so a business structure is an absolute must to put in place early.

If you are doing everything within your business, then the structure will be simple, but that will not always be the case. The chances are at some point, you will have people involved who you envisage as future partners or investors in the business.

The general business structure options are:

- Sole trader

- Limited liability company (LLC)

- Proprietary limited company (Pty Limited)

- Trust

Each of these entities has various risks that you would be wise to work through with an accounting specialist who understands the upside and downside for each.

The most common structure is a company, be it LLC or Pty Limited. A trust is an interesting structure that requires an appointee and a trustee, a role often fulfilled by a registered company. The last three structures each need written constitutions and beneficiaries in place to remove ambiguity around managing the raft of administrative formalities that go with the territory. Distributions, shareholding agreements, taxation and, in the case of Australia, payroll tax and superannuation are all matters of vital importance that would benefit from expert help.

Oftentimes, this type of work is a prerequisite for starting a distillery, applying for capital funding, attracting investors and satisfying the various licencing requirements. Best speak with a specialist and seek professional advice from the start. Yep, that means finding your favourite lawyer and accountant.

Summary

- Your business may start off as a flight of fancy, but if you really want to pursue it, that needs to translate into a clear and comprehensive business plan.

- Understand the real motivations behind wanting to start a distillery.

- Always start with the end in mind. How will you exit your business?

- Consider where you will locate your business, taking into account the existing infrastructure and anything else that could impact on your intended premises.

- Take into account the costs of making good if you decide to lease.

- Make sure wherever you choose has the space you will need to operate.

- There are key considerations for a distillery location, such as good power and water supply. Make yourself aware of these and look for them in the locations you view.

- Select the largest capacity, highest quality still you can afford to buy right now and review it annually to make sure it meets your business's expanding requirements.

- What equipment other than the still will you need in your premises? What can you acquire later and what do you need right now?

- What suppliers are there in your area?

- Now is the time to start building a good relationship with still fabricators. This relationship will last a lifetime – and may even span generations.

- How will you structure your business? A company, LLC or Pty Limited is the most common choice.

- Employ expert help at every stage of your business plan to ensure you consider everything. It is money well spent.

5

Compliance

Compliance is an enormous subject worthy of its own book, but the general premise may be summarised under three broad headings:

- Safety, health and environment (SHE) – plant, people, equipment, environment; compliance with AS1940 and other relevant industry legislation.

- Revenue – for example, excise, goods and services tax (GST)/value-added tax (VAT)/sales tax treatments and reporting; compliance with the Australian Corporations Act,[63] taxation laws, GST collection. In Australia, there are also the joys of business activity statements and payroll tax thrown in for good measure.

- Accountability – company directors, management, personnel; compliance with corporate governance, equal employment opportunities and nondiscriminatory employment.

With respect to location and approvals to manufacture, the agencies that are most likely to consider issues with an open mind are at local government/ local council level, with a particular emphasis on safety. Be aware, though, that differences in location can present nuances specific to the area. Here are two classic examples from 2021 where a council response to what I thought was a simple question left me confused:

Q: How do I secure a liquor licence for my business?

A planning permit may be required for a liquor licence depending on the type of licence required.

This was an answer I didn't expect to a question I hadn't asked. The response suggested that I needed to ask clearer, more specific questions.

Q: How do I start my distilling business at home?

Provided the home-based business requirements at clause 52.11 are met, no planning permit is required for the use under the General Residential Zone.

Experience suggests to me that this is how this would play out. I'd learn later that I'd need to separate my house from where I intend to distil, preferably in another building that may need to comply with a planning permit requirement.

> **PRO TIP**
>
> Think about the requirements you would need to design and build an industrial kitchen, at home or in a restaurant. This ought to give you an insight into the planning permissions you will need to consider for a distillery.

The solution may sound like a garage. Perhaps. Or perhaps not. Note that the advice doesn't describe any workable options that would satisfy a council, because it's up to you to find out what they are. You won't be told by the council. It's only when you present your case that you will discover if your choice was wise or not. Can you meet the storage and handling requirements for managing alcohol products safely? Remember, it's all about safety first, so take that into account.

As always, seek advice on the best way to proceed. Start a meaningful relationship with the town planner and key decision makers in your local government body as soon as practicable.

Local government

The future success of your distillery hangs off the prudent selection of an appropriate location of sufficient size to site your operations. Check with your local council about the suitability of the location you have chosen and see if any prior applications in the area were unsuccessful. There will be documented reasons behind the decision, so unleash your inner sleuth and find out why.

Council is a British term that describes local government and the bureaucracy used to operate it 'successfully'. It is maintained by councillors and other officials whose role may seem to be to stop you at any cost and prevent you from progressing with your craft distillery plans. Remember, their responses, albeit frustrating, are well intended.

These are the people you need to make your best friends. Not Facebook friends, but real friends: people you visit, call regularly, invest time in, understand, listen to with your fullest attention.

The number of decision makers who successfully confuse distillery, winery and brewery founders is remarkable, but they are often the same folks who know the difference between whisky, wine and beer. Go figure! Few councils want a distillery on their patch; that is the general default position to expect, and that is just the start. Be prepared to hunker down and dig in for a protracted engagement. This is why establishing a strong relationship with your local council officials from the start is essential.

To make things even more interesting, two different councils may consider your distillery setup compliance requirements differently. In some cases, distillery setups in the same local government/local council may be treated differently as well.

There are exceptions, of course. For Australian readers, a notable one is South Australia (SA). The SA tourist sector has recognised the attraction of distillery visits, and authorities appreciate that distilleries generate jobs, sell product and the local government recoups their cut – everyone wins.

So why *are* council approvals so devilishly difficult to secure?

Challenges to prepare for

Inexperience

Chances are the local government you need to approach will have no experience whatsoever with the requirements of a distillery. This makes perfect sense. If we consider Australia as an example, there are about 300 craft distilleries, spread across six states and two territories occupying some 7.692 million km^2.

The chance of landing on a local council with distillery experience within that geographical range is slim.

Self-preservation

When confronted with something as readily misunderstood and leftfield as a distillery, many council officials view taking on an enterprise of this nature as a tad risky. Bear in mind, too, that public servants are often risk averse and may be unwilling to upset people with this strange 'thing'.

Assumed knowledge

The term 'distillery' conjures up all sorts of images for people in council, the majority of which will not match your vision or intent at all. The terms 'factory', 'manufacturing plant' or 'food manufacturer' are more readily understood, but if you resort to these, the difficulty comes when you reply to a legitimate question concerning what you intend to make.

Can you imagine the shock and horror?

'But you said you were a food manufacturer!'

'You said you were a factory, you didn't say you were making moonshine in a shed.'

'Um, that's because I'm not…'

When you are working with people who are not distillery specialists, you will need to educate them – and you, too, will have a learning opportunity. The councillor will possess bureaucratic knowledge, albeit probably in a field completely unrelated to distilling. Between the two of you, an interesting ballroom two-step will unfold. It may be awkward at first, but stick with it and you'll be tripping the light fantastic in the end.

CASE STUDY – THE CITY OF LONDON DISTILLERY

An enterprising gentleman by the name of Jonathan Clarke owned a cocktail bar on Bride Lane and sought to bring back distilling to the heart of London after an absence of some 200 years.[64] Why so long? Famine, taxation and government regulation took their toll upon the Gin Craze, bringing it to an end.

Given the history and connection that London has with gin, surely rejuvenating the art of distilling right in the middle of the city would be a relatively straightforward process? I guess you can work out the answer.

No one in local government had any experience with this type of development approval – one of the by-products of the 200-year absence. That meant Jonathan had to start from scratch. In so doing, he enlisted help from one of the world's foremost experts in craft distilling setups, the Artisan Distiller Jamie Baxter.[65]

The journey from concept to commercialisation took eighteen months, exhausting the original project budget at around the twelve-month mark. After that, six months of creative entrepreneurship helped cash flow, guiding the venture to a successful launch.

CASE STUDY – SIX STRING BREWING

In 2010, Chris Benson and his business partner Adam Klasterka had a simple idea: 'Let's bring craft beer to our local community on the Central Coast of NSW, Australia.'[66] When they decided to realise their vision, little did they know that the next three years would be fraught with council battles, guaranteed to test the mettle of anyone to its limits.

In no specific order, their quest for a location encompassed:

- Three different sites, including one body corporate that wrote new bylaws prohibiting the sale of alcohol on the site, even though the previous tenant was another type of brewery
- Battles with planning permission
- Bureaucracy
- Council bylaws
- Public opposition from figures in the community

The message from opponents was simple, and is probably familiar to distillers everywhere:

'No, you can't. Not here.'

Chris and Adam saw things differently. They organised a survey to garner support for the brewery, which delivered a resounding message:

'Yes, you can. Right here.'

In a shout out to their tenacity and unbridled passion, their enthusiasm was undimmed by the opposition and energised by the level of support they were generating. Their protracted campaign led to a victory three years down the track, when Six String Brewery opened its doors to the public for the first time.

Since launching, the brewery has gone from strength to strength with expansion plans to include its first foray into craft spirits. Brewers bring a wealth of technical and enterprise experience that can only benefit the craft spirits fraternity.

Licences

Make sure that you get all of these under control and on display. Jurisdictions around the world will differ, so it is best to seek advice from one of the many supporting associations that exist for craft distillers.

In Australia, the licences you need for starters are:

- Licence to manufacture excisable products – alcohol[67]

- Permission – still[68]

- Excise licences – alcohol[69]

- Under bond storage licence[70]

These licences can form part of your discussion with the local council.

Distilling in New Zealand

New Zealand is the only jurisdiction in the world where you do not require a licence to own or operate a still. This has implications for excise tax. In the NZ Customs Act 1996, Excise Regulation 9 states that: 'Any person who produces beer, wine or spirits for his or her own consumption is exempt from excise tax.'[71]

There is also an exemption from the manufacturing area licencing requirement if you use any part of your private house or land to grow tobacco for your own use.

'Personal use' may be subject to interpretation, but taken prima facie, this means that you may not sell spirits you've distilled, nor – interestingly – give it away. To do so would be illegal under the act unless you were to satisfy the licencing requirements under the Sale and Supply of Liquor Act 2012 permitting the sale of spirits.[72]

This was not always the case, though. Prior to 1996, under the customs act, distilling alcohol required a licence and attracted excise, but policing home stills for small amounts of alcohol proved to be neither cost effective nor efficient because:

- The maximum fine under the act was $500

- Transgressors had their alcohol confiscated, which on a domestic scale did not amount to a great deal

- The confiscated spirits would need safe disposal, at a cost

- Prosecution costs in the thousands of dollars outweighed the benefit of a successfully upheld case

Public lobbying of MPs drove changes to the customs act in the 1990s. The act now includes the word spirits, which – along with brewing beer or growing tobacco – does not attract excise tax if it's for your own use.

CASE STUDY – EXCISE IN AUSTRALIA

Australia is ascribed in its national anthem as a land where 'We are one and free'. A sunburnt country, girt by sea. Most of the population lives on the eastern coastal fringe. It is the home of some of the world's deadliest critters, both land loving and aquatic. It is also home to more than 300 active craft distilleries, up from thirty-eight in 2014.[73]

Most of Australia's distilleries are in rural areas where the economies are fragile and employment opportunities are scarce. Distilleries there are playing their part in addressing both challenges. This sterling work takes place against an economic background where the spirits industry carries the third highest excise rate on the planet,[74] surpassed only by Iceland and Norway.

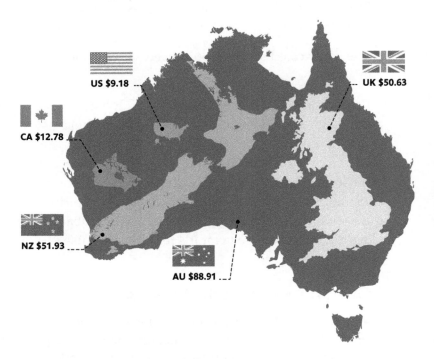

Not only that, but the excise undergoes arbitrary increases every six months. At the current rate of progress, this could be another critter to add to Australia's list of most deadly.

Prior to May 2021, Australia had an excise rebate scheme through which $AUD100k paid would result in the government returning $AUD60k in a given financial year. These arrangements changed in May 2021, with the government now returning $AUD350k to distilleries, a welcome boost for an industry whose best is to come.

If the good people of Australia can find ways to establish their operations in testing economic conditions (drought, bushfire threat, flooding), take confidence in your ability to solve the economic challenges that will come your way. Excise is a true variable cost for your operations to cater for in your business plan.

Summary

- Compliance, a huge subject, can be summarised under three broad headings in the context of starting a distillery: safety, health and environment; revenue; and accountability.

- Before you present your case for starting a distillery in a particular location, be sure to find out what requirements you'll need to meet.

- Seek advice on the best way to proceed by starting a meaningful relationship with the town planner and key decision makers in your local government.

- Gaining approval from local councils for your distillery can be devilishly difficult, so be prepared.

- Many local councils have no experience of awarding permissions to distillers, so you may need to educate them on what you're all about. Take this as an opportunity to learn about bureaucracy from them, too.

- There will be support for your venture, even if at first it seems like everyone is against you. Get out in the community and rally that support – you're likely to need it.

- Make sure that you get all requisite licences on display. Jurisdictions around the world will differ, so seek advice from one of the many associations that exist to support craft distillers.

- Cater for the variable cost of excise in your business plan.

6

Operations

The term 'operations' can conjure up all sorts of imagery, ranging from a scalpel-wielding surgeon with rubber gloves to a group of soldiers readying for an assault upon an enemy enclave.

Pleasingly, the meaning of operations in a craft distillery is nowhere near as scary as either of these. According to the *American Production and Inventory Control Society Dictionary*, 15th edition,[75] operations comprises 'The group that produces the goods and/or services that a company sells'.

Simple. It's the people in the distillery who safely make the stuff intended for sale. Who exactly are these people and what do you expect them to do?

Your people

The easiest way to visualise an answer to these questions – other than visiting a distillery during bottling day – is to go to a Subway store.[76] The reason I have suggested Subway is solely to do with the manufacturing process it uses to create its products, and it happens right in front of you.

Here is how I've taken Subway operations and nominated the equivalents from a distillery operations viewpoint:

Subway operation	Distillery operation	Distillery role
Bread selection	Distilled product	Distiller
Product selection	Reduced and filtered product	Vat controller
Filling selections	Bottle filling	Filler operator
Cutting (if needed)	Bottle closures	Filler operator
Wrapping	Bottle labelling	Packing operator
Handover	Bottle packing	Packing operator
Financial transaction	Bottle orders	Despatch operator

At low demand times, a single Subway sandwich artist (yep, that is what they're called) can manage all the operations on their own. When demand increases, additional sandwich artists make their way into the assembly line and the division of labour kicks in to provide great customer service.

In many ways, your distillery operations will follow a similar workflow. You are likely to be the sole 'spirit artist' covering off the distiller, vat controller, filling, packing and despatching roles in the first instance. Just like the Subway assembly model, you can then consider roles in your production line that warrant additional pairs of hands – artists, if you will – to provide excellent customer service.

It is highly likely that you – or someone who can legally drive a vehicle – will have to do the despatching to start with, delivering the bottles of your pride and joy personally. Delivery, of course, may include packing up goods for posting from a post office, or via some other delivery process that best supports your business.

The secret sauce in this method is simple. You now have a good idea of the various operations that you need to cover so that you can despatch your goods. The best thing to do is to figure out ways to delegate operational tasks as quickly as possible so that you can focus on supplying great craft spirits for sale. Regardless of the scale of your operation, the functions listed in the table will need catering for. Adding in people as you need them will do the trick in the early days, but they will reach their operational capacity far faster than you may expect. Plan for future capacity now.

How many people do I add?

A word of caution. There is a tipping point: a critical mass that occurs when the number of additional folks will hinder your quest for greater output.

Consider this. A team of three has three communication channels. Each person can speak to two others and vice versa; me talking to you uses the same 'channel' as you talking to me.

A team of five has ten communication channels. The addition of two extra people has more than tripled the number of channels. This provides opportunities for messages, instructions and intentions to be lost, misheard, misunderstood and generally screwed up with little effort at all.

This is manageable, of course, by you in the first instance, and then through leadership by example, but you cannot keep doing this when you have products to sell and a business to run.

Delegation needs to be your operations superpower from the outset. Allow delegation to occupy pride of place in the strategic thinking you apply throughout your craft spirits journey.

Choosing your team

When it comes to team, choosing the best people to meet your business needs can be challenging. Surely no one can do things better than you? Ask yourself that question in an empty room and count the number of people brave enough to disagree with you. That is the curse.

Choosing your team becomes even more complicated if the people you have in mind are close friends or family that you have never worked with before. When you are finding your own feet, one of the more interesting things will be the array of people who want to help you. What is equally interesting is the number of people you already know and would like to have on board, but then you find they do not share your vision. In fact, they may be antagonistic toward the whole idea.

When I posed these scenarios to a mentor of mine, his reply was crystal clear. According to his sage advice, there are seven distinct groups of people that you may encounter throughout your craft spirits journey. At the start, there will be a sense of camaraderie and energy associated with a kick-off enterprise that has so many pleasing social elements to it. The general well-trodden approach is to engage with people you are familiar with and feel you can trust. Also consider engaging with people who play to your strengths and can shore up the areas of your business which are not strongpoints. They may be people who are near and dear to you; they may be family; they may be friends of friends, but the chances are you will be able to group them into one of these seven categories. As harsh as it sounds, especially when you're considering friends, it's worth writing down a list of candidates and deciding which group they would fit in to.

In no particular order:

- Group 1 are people inspired by your awesomeness

- Group 2 will resent your success, and you

- Group 3 will want the results you achieve without exerting any effort themselves

- Group 4 will arrive late to the party and expect to take over from you

- Group 5 will be pleased for you and form your cheer squad

- Group 6 will love you and what you do, but want to compete with you

- Group 7 will appear from out of the blue with random acts of kindness and a genuine desire to help you succeed

Loosely, we have missionaries, mercenaries and misfits. Sound familiar?

You may already be aware of people among your friends, family and acquaintances who fit into one of these groups. The challenge is to carefully select those who will help you do the job you have signed up for. If you are in any doubt what your job is, it is this.

Whether you like it or not, you are the CEO of your business. The CEO's job, if you were running a public-listed business, would be to deliver the business plan. Your job in your business, even if it is just you – and usually it *is* just you until the cavalry arrives – is to deliver the business plan. All people you bring in and activities you perform or delegate need alignment with that single goal.

Be specific at the start about how many products you want to sell. Be clear about the number of units for each product you intend to sell – and therefore make – and how many people you need to do that.

Gino Wickman's superb book *Traction*[77] refers to a simple concept. It can be hard to apply at different stages of your craft spirits journey, but at some point, this will be a key insight when tackling team-related matters:

Get the right people in the right seats.

According to *Traction*, there are at least two to start with: an integrator to get shit done and a visionary to think about the future outcomes for the business in a given timeframe. In my experience, there is also a third function. In the Four Pillars Gin model, for example, there is one who makes the noise (the visionary), one who makes the gin (the integrator) and one who makes sense (the mediator).[78] From humble beginnings in 2013 to Global Business of the Year in 2019 and 2020, Four Pillars and its model, it's fair to say, are working well.

The right people are those who fit and thrive in the business culture you are looking to create. The right seat means that people are operating to their strengths in the enterprise. In sporting parlance, people fill positions on the team that play to their unique abilities. Few inside linebackers make great quarterbacks in an American football team, for example.

Looking back at our 'Subwayed' operations model, we see five functions that need catering for in a distillery: distiller, vat controller, filler, packer and despatcher. Early on, you will be doing everything, but as soon as you feel there is an operation you can delegate, think about the seven groups, the right people and the right seats for them to occupy.

This approach will become increasingly important as your business grows, co-ordination efforts require more input, sales demand rises, and you need more of everything and for everyone to get on top of it all quickly. It is a never-ending challenge that goes with growth; and the time to think about growth is at the start with the business plan. Why would you want your business to be doing anything other than growing, right?

The four steps of effective delegation

Like many people who want to embark on a journey into distilling, you may find it easy to fall into the trap of believing you'll be doing everything yourself, forever and ever. There is a degree of satisfaction to this approach, albeit a short-lived one. Once the novelty wears off, the last thing you want to happen is to feel that you've traded in your former steady job for a different job without the rewards, but with a truckload more stress than before.

This is where delegation is key.

According to business leader Tim Dwyer in his 2017 podcast with Glen Carlson,[79] there are three types of work. A good tip is to apply a colour scheme to your calendar to see your differing work allocations:

- Red work – low value, administrative in nature

- Blue work – vital for business success, eg sales and delivery

- Black work – high value, eg looking to the future

The amount of time you spend in each of these areas will differ during the journey. Suffice to say, black work rules at the start, blue work rules once you're underway. A mixture of all three will occupy the spaces in between.

Making this distinction is vital for a craft spirits business. It will help you prioritise what you need to spend your time doing and what you can outsource to others.

I've often heard people say that they've 'tried' delegation, but it didn't work, so it was 'easier' to do it all themselves. This is a classic example of short-term gain, long-term pain, though few ever frame this everyday situation in such terms.

Instead of getting caught up with this suboptimal approach, you can follow four key steps to effective delegation – and no, delegation doesn't mean you run away and leave people to it. Remember, it's more about the delegator than the person you are delegating to. You're still accountable for the outcome.

Step one: The outcome

Clearly define your desired goal. What will be the ultimate success measure? Then you can communicate...

Step two: The way you like things

Train your folks concerning any odd-ball process preferences that you have, eg label orientation, box stacking on a pallet, a sharpie or a blue pen on shipper labels. Whatever these idiosyncrasies are, tell people.

Step three: Tools

Set your people up with all the tools, resources and/or support they are going to need in advance. If they need a cork mallet, get one; if they need packing tape and machines, get them; if they need buckets and cleaning gear for end of day 'clean in place' processes (CIPs), get them. If they run out of labels or other packing materials, that is on you, not the assignee, unless you've told them what to do in advance. You, and only you, are accountable for the success or failure of the people you delegate to.

Step four: Trust

Delegate responsibility and authority, not just the task. Have a completion deadline or review time, then get out of the assignees' way and leave them well alone.

This is the best short-term pain, long-term gain approach you can take. Embrace it as soon as you can to make your operations fun, effective, accurate and controllable.

If you are still unconvinced, bear this mind. There are four levels of competence whenever delegation comes to the fore.[80] Consider an occasion when you need to train someone for a task you can do without effort; one where you are unconsciously competent.

At first, the assignee is acutely aware that they cannot do the same task, yet. They are **unconsciously incompetent** and struggling. Your expectations are unmet, you feel you are going backward, and you may lose patience and decide it's quicker and easier to do it yourself.

At level 2, the assignee is struggling, only this time, they are clear about the areas where they're struggling. They are **consciously incompetent** and ask for help. You can then review your approach with the assignee, committing to working through the challenges with a focus on the outcome.

Level 3 occurs when the assignee has worked through the challenging areas with you and can confidently complete the delegated task, albeit with a few guides along the way. The assignee is now **consciously competent**, and with time and practice, they will become as **unconsciously competent** at the task as you are. You are no longer going backward; you've built trust and created additional capacity in your business. With the extra time that's now available to you, you can invest in other areas that need attention.

Remember, you make money *selling* craft spirits, not making them. The sooner you can delegate operational activities to others, the sooner you will have capacity to focus on the selling process.

The sales and operations plan

A sales and operations plan? What is that?

Basically, it is piecing together all plans from each of your business functions in ways that balance what you intend to sell with what you need to make for whom and when.

Consider planning a three-course meal for twelve at your house. Think about all the things you need to organise, and pretty soon you will see how this can translate into an example of a sales and operations plan.

Your guests are your customers, sales and marketing activity concerns invitations, product development refers to the dishes you intend to serve, manufacturing refers to preparing the food in sufficient quantities for your guests to consume. There is a planning and scheduling side to this as well, as you will serve the dishes one by one, not all at once. Material sourcing refers to considering the quantities of any ingredients you already have, and then working out what you need to source, and finance refers to the amount of money you would like to spend. You may even have requests for an additional guest or two or last-minute cancellations to contend with.

Apply this to production operations in your craft distillery as well. Forecast what you intend to sell, procure bottles, labels, closures in sufficient quantities to meet the sales plans, manage your inventory so that you have materials in stock if a rush order comes along. These quantities are referred to as safety stock and trigger the need to order more materials when quantities reach a designated low limit. There is a fair amount of science behind this, balancing supply lead time, cost per unit and a concept called minimum order quantity.

Third-party distilling

Third-party distilling is a great option for any startup operation to consider. The best way to frame it is to view it with a branding, sales and marketing lens first and foremost. It is unlikely to generate great profit, but it will give you an accelerated route to market that would otherwise be hindered by the lack of plant, equipment, location, licences and skilled personnel who love the idea as much as you do.

Product, brand and marketing, and distribution are the key cash drivers in any business, and this comes acutely into focus when you're considering a product to make, sell and deliver. None of these cash drivers are easy to do, but product is best considered to be the 'least difficult'. To simplify the product part of the equation further, you can consider getting a third party to make it for you.

There are a few requirements to consider when you're enlisting help from third parties. This is not a comprehensive list, merely covering off the basics of product components and financial implications, but it will also apply when you intend to start producing, selling and distributing from your own facility. Based on the sales performance of your products, you may need to reconsider the plant's planned capacity. Do you scale up, scale down or leave your initial assumptions unchanged? Or your analysis and review may prompt you to enter into a longer-term partnership arrangement with a third-party distiller.

Now let's have a look at those requirements. Take examples of your ideal product with you as a benchmark to share with your prospective partner. Make sure they provide you with legitimate cost estimates based upon the litres of pure alcohol forecast.

Include the estimate cost of raw materials before you distil (or ferment as the case may be). Ask for the details in an easy-to-understand format – Excel is perfect – so you can model outcomes based upon your business plan. The key preparation steps are to determine what the cost of goods sold (COGS) will be for the product you intend to bottle, sell and ship.

Confirm these costs in a single reference sheet:

- Bottling costs
- Minimum bottle quantities and bottle size
- Dry goods (bottles, labels, closures, shippers)
- Excise and other taxes
- Labour costs and manufacturing overheads

You really need to know what your full COGS will be at the bottled product point.

Tie your prospective partner to delivery dates so you can plan delivery and pricing with wholesalers, distribution and retail channels. Be sure you both understand what the arrangement will include and not include.

For example, your prospective partner may create the liquid, pack it into 20-litre/5-gallon food-grade drums, and then ship it to you for packaging in your own time. Alternatively, they may ferment a wash, distil that wash, reduce to strength, fill, cap, label and pack for you.

Confirm the outcomes of your negotiation in writing. This needs to include the cost, the bill of materials involved and the date you can expect to take receipt of the product.

In many ways, the steps you need to take are no different to asking any skilled tradesman to deliver a product or service to your home. You'll have a budget based upon research, you'll have clear and unambiguous views about the product outcomes you expect, and the hired help will be able to tell you whether they can do the job or not.

CASE STUDY – SA DISTILLING CO

Heaps Good Gin[81] is SA Distilling Company's flagship product. It is the pride and joy of founders Marcelle McEwan and Greg Nunan.

Marcelle's career experience is diverse, ranging from the culinary arts to debt recovery. Greg has a background in digital marketing. It became clear to them early in their business development phase, that product development was an area that needed attention, but by their own assessment, it didn't play to their individual or collective strengths.

Seeking help from third-party producers made perfect sense. The advantages lay solely in prioritising the three cash drivers. By outsourcing product development, they could then focus on brand marketing and distribution.

The gin's name pays homage to a quintessentially South Australian vernacular that describes someone, something or an event in terms that significantly exceed one's expectations. The company's narrative is proudly

South Australian, for South Australia, based on things South Australian. The company's focus is on the use of local botanicals wherever possible, engaging local suppliers and packaging expertise. The branding used these elements as key building blocks to support the product launch in May 2021.

Both Marcelle and Greg share more of their insights for people starting on their own craft spirits journey via the *Still Magic* podcast.[82]

In many ways, using a third-party producer brings the notion of craft distilling more closely within reach, freeing up time to consider other business elements.

Summary

- Using the 'Subway table', consider the roles you'll need to cover in your distillery business, and start planning to fill those roles right from the start.

- With reference to the seven groups detailed in this chapter, work out where each of the people you're considering for your team falls. Basically, are they missionaries, mercenaries or misfits?

- Remember, it is your job to deliver the business plan.

- When choosing your team, get the right people in the right seats, ie playing to their strengths.

- Embrace delegation. This is your secret sauce to long-term success, starting with operations.

- Make sure those your delegate to are clear on what you expect from them. Their success is in your hands.

- Design your sales and operations plan.

- Consider third parties to accelerate product development and speed to market, leaving you free to concentrate on the other two cash drivers.

7

Putting The Business Plan Together

This section has stressed the importance of a business plan, but if you have never written one before, what does it resemble and how do you determine what good looks like? And if you know that much, how do you bridge the gap between good and not?

Let us explore these questions in a little more detail.

You now know that your job is to deliver the business plan. This means you need to know what tasks must get done, the skillsets required to do them and the best order in which to tackle them. Consider key factors such as location, affordability and a clear sense of purpose. How hard can it be?

There is only so much cognitive capacity available to a single person, so drawing up and executing your business plan alone is a tough way to go about it. Unless you are hell-bent on doing everything yourself, delegating parts of the design and execution of the plan to others is a smart use of key resources: people, time and finance. This will give you the capacity to work on your great art, play to your strengths and bolster areas where you need help.

A good analogy is house building. Few people have all the skills required to build a house on their own. Instead, they employ the services of qualified architects and surveyors, maybe a lawyer to deal with all the legal considerations. Then for the house build itself, they find skilled bricklayers, plumbers, roofers, carpenters, electricians… the list goes on.

So it is with creating a craft spirits business. If you count the number of manufacturing facilities in your locality and compare that figure with the number of distilleries in the same area, you will see how rare the latter is. This sets context. Your call to adventure will be epic, your own hero's journey. A business plan, well-crafted and executed by you and the right people to support you, will help you make it to the end.

Business plan themes

According to Robert T Kiyosaki, 'A successful business is created before there is a business.'[83]

Knowing what to write, what to start with and how to express these concepts clearly in your business plan is a skill. An adage implies that everyone has a book inside them; the difficulty is extricating it.

Here are some themes that warrant thought throughout the business plan creation process:

- **Be bold.** Plan for the business to grow without you. In other words, consider what your own exit strategy will be, right from the start.

- **Make your ambitions the business's lifeblood.** Consider this theme as you work through your business plan at the beginning, and continue to refine what your ambitions will resemble over time. If your ambition is clear, the reasons why you're going into the distilling industry will be easy to understand, and if you know what needs doing, then people will want to be part of your vision. Success is extremely attractive.

- **Customers are key.** Make working with your business a great experience from order placement to consumption. Aim for great products, delivered in full, on time, every time.

- **Create a strong team.** That means parking your ego and exercising delegation. Think in terms of product, brand and marketing, and distribution, and the skills needed make these happen.

- **Be a good guardian of the planet.** Consider the environment in all your dealings and make sure that your business aims include leaving the planet in a better place than when you started. Think about how you will treat trade waste, spent botanicals, water use, energy supply and consumption, recyclable materials, used barrels and packaging materials.

- **Enjoy yourself.** Business is hard. It becomes doubly hard if you do not enjoy what you do in pursuit of your ambitions. Never lose sight of this. Your sense of purpose is your best ally.

- **Create, adhere to and publicise your values.** Values provide an operating framework for your business that defines which behaviours are OK and which are not.

Here are a few examples of values from well-known brands:

- Juno Gin: 'Make it right.'[84]

- Still Magic: 'Heritage. Guardianship. Legacy.'

- Jack Daniels: 'Independence. Integrity. Authenticity.'[85]

Sample structure

The table below provides some key headings for a solid business plan. Each of these summarises work that needs analysis and expression. The good news is that if you embrace your new superpower, delegation, you may be able to section out this work for others to do. IT project managers writing plans, construction engineers writing scope documents or tenders and financial folks crafting business cases will be familiar with this cornerstone document. If there is someone in your network who shares your vision and can articulate this in a business plan, get them on board as soon as you can. At some point, recruitment and selection are going to be part of the journey, so get on to it early.

CASE STUDY – REEFTON DISTILLING CO.

Reefton Distilling Co., a craft distillery in Aotearoa, are the creators of Little Biddy Gin. The founder and chief executive, Patsy Bass, invested many hours into business plans for different types of business before deciding upon a distillery project.

Seeing the indicators for growth in the sector, private equity enabled Bass to take an idea to a NZ$10m business and their Little Biddy Gin to the number two super-premium gin in New Zealand in two years.

At year three, further investment was sought to accelerate growth, setting the business value at NZ$26m (US$18m).

Business plan section	Purpose	Best person for the job
Executive summary	Describes why and how you intend to conduct business, what you intend to produce and with whom	You or a business partner
Company profile	Demonstrates values, positioning, structure, intentions	You or a business partner
Industry analysis	Examines strengths, weaknesses, opportunities and threats, industry trends. Options analysis. Gap analysis. Target definition. Size of the prize	You or a business partner
Product strategy	Demonstrates that your product or products satisfy the business plan's objectives	A product expert who can translate your intent into a working strategy
Brand strategy	Demonstrates that your branding components align with the product and business plan's objectives	Brand expert who can translate your business intent into strategy

Business plan section	Purpose	Best person for the job
Marketing strategy	Demonstrates that your marketing strategy is consistent with the product and branding strategy and intent in the business plan	Marketing expert who can translate business intent into strategy
Distribution strategy	Demonstrates that you have considered the best way to supply product to your customers, in full, on time, every time	An expert who understands distribution functions and can translate that into a strategy for your business
Operations plan	Demonstrates that plant, equipment and personnel can legally function effectively and safely to support the business plan. This includes identifying and securing all licences, satisfying all compliance requirements, sourcing complaint plant and equipment, engaging expert help, shop floor reporting (eg safety reporting, manning levels, dry and wet goods inventory, finished goods inventory, production output, measuring and accounting for all litres of liquid alcohol consumed or packaged, cycle counts, purchase requisitions)	Operations expert with experience in manufacturing fast-moving consumer goods safely and legally in a compliant location

Continued

Cont.

Business plan section	Purpose	Best person for the job
Business growth strategy	Articulates best-case, most-likely-case and worst-case scenarios for the business, based upon contemporaneous information as it comes to hand	Business development expert with industry experience
Financial plan	Demonstrates that you have taken capital and operational expense into account and can support reporting requirements for internal (team and partners) and external (excise authorities) parties	Finance expert with skills in cost analysis, profitability, financial reporting (cash flow, profit and loss, balance sheet) and forecasting
Exit strategy	Describes the future vision of the business (sustaining, expansion, diversification, divestment) and the roles people may fulfil in each scenario	You and your partners

The business plan will need diagrams, summary tables and references to relevant materials. This will help those reading it for the first time and identify content gaps you may need to fill. Cater for the fact that your business plan's content will be read by different audiences, ranging from potential partners to subject-matter experts and government agencies (local, regional or national) that issue licences to support your craft spirits manufacturing efforts.

That is right: anyone who is anyone will want to know what you're up to. These same folks will be willing and enthusiastic to provide feedback about the areas you need to fix up. Criticism, constructive or otherwise, is far easier to supply than creativity, and they will likely delight in doing so. As tough as it can be, take the feedback in good faith and apply, review or rule it out as you see fit.

A word of caution, though. Incorporate all feedback from government agencies as you implement business plan changes and recommendations.

CASE STUDY - STUART MACKENZIE, LITTLE JUNIPER DISTILLING

Stuart Mackenzie started Little Juniper Distilling in 2020,[86] choosing an urban location in his home city of Adelaide, SA. Stuart's plan and passion for creating a distillery had been a long-term goal, but one that remained latent for some time.[87] Given Stuart's successful career to date, spanning the computer game industry, visual effects for Hollywood movies, marketing, advertising and web design, this was an offbeat ambition.

In and around 2018, Stuart was considering a campaign lasting between five and ten years, but he had started his business plan well before then – then the COVID-19 pandemic struck.

Interestingly, Stuart's response to COVID was to accelerate the distillery business plan. The result? After three weeks of nine-hour days, five days a week, he had a 102-page document, replete with tables to present data, equipment requirements, safety needs, licencing and other requirements, and a twenty-four-page Excel financial plan designed to work out all profits and expenses for two years as a key supporting document.

Stuart says, 'A solid and detailed business plan lets you see into the future and plan for any contingencies, makes you accountable while setting realistic goals, and is your road map.'

The best part of all? The Australian Tax Office was so impressed, an official rang Stuart personally to thank him for the best business plan they'd ever seen and grant him his licence to manufacture.

Summary

- At risk of repeating this *ad nauseam*, your job is to deliver the business plan. It's that important.

- Get help to write your plan when you need it as a matter of priority.

- The business plan needs to include references to the cash drivers (product, brand / marketing, distribution).

- Different audiences (legislators, future partners, 'tyre kickers') will consume your business plan content. Use this fact to your advantage, but make sure it's written in a clear way that's accessible to every interested party.

- Engage trusted partners or expert help to review it with you.

- Use the feedback you get, both constructive and otherwise, to help refine your plan.

- Some feedback you may choose to ignore, but always take on board that from government agencies.

Congratulations! You now have the backbone of your future distillery business: the business plan. It's now time to examine the three cash drivers that will take your business from surviving to thriving.

PART THREE

THE CASH DRIVERS

8

Product

People intending to embark on a craft spirits journey are oftentimes those who already make things for others to use or consume. The craft spirits industry is replete with folks from backgrounds in the culinary arts, engineering, music, boiler making, theatre, working on Hollywood blockbuster movies and everything else in between. Making things is best described in a craft spirits context as 'operations', which we covered in Chapter 6.

Let's take a look at what you need to make a product you can be proud of.

Product strategy

Strategy? Who knew that making stuff is something other than a willy-nilly set of activities that you suddenly decide is a good idea to pursue?

You may have the best product idea since sliced bread, but if people are not particularly fussed about your clever addition of pecans, or even sliced bread in general, then you may find yourself in a wee tangle holding lots of lovingly made product that no one wants. Here is the good news – the opportunity for craft spirit makers lies in one large, profitable and extremely popular product type.

You, my friend, are going to focus your efforts in the ever-expanding super-premium plus market. Super-premium plus means fewer quantities, higher quality and higher margins. The IWSR defines super-premium plus by price.[88]

In my view, there will be heightened focus upon provenance and sustainability as USPs. This is good news for those of you wanting to know what to make, how to enrich your narrative as a maker and whom to target.

This brings your strategy into focus. Do you make eCommerce the key route to market, supplying small quantities of high-value items for a longer period than you may originally have planned? Can you challenge the role that traditional distributors and wholesalers provide?

Distributors and wholesalers are likely to consider enhanced eCommerce and digital strategies themselves to help them work more closely with producers, other distributors and retail chains. This will likely include some form of drop shipping (delivering goods directly from the manufacturer to the customer) or several hubs in future.

CASE STUDY – SOLVING PRODUCT SALES CHALLENGES IN PNG

PNG is the land of the unexpected, a mixture of the beautiful and the brutal, home to 6 million people and 850 languages. With so many languages in play, you can probably imagine that there are opportunities for misunderstanding between people.

During my time in PNG, a few reality checks kicked in. Most of the people in my manufacturing team spoke a minimum of five different languages. Oftentimes, this meant that English was either their fourth or fifth language, which was a challenge, given that English was the language of commerce. The first step for me was to find a common language to bridge the gap. Lessons in Tok Pisin – the everyday language in PNG – was the solution.

The written word was always going to be challenging for people to understand, regardless of the message intent, so the leadership team brought in skilled sign writers to create industrial-scale hoardings and advertising images. There was an existing operational capacity in the plant, so the goal was to create a safer, more efficient workplace and give the operational leads greater autonomy. Safety, standardised packaging, operating procedures, adherence to quality measures were key.

As a team, we created our own simple branding, logos and pricing structures to support new product launches. Finance, Operations, Sales and Marketing were at the table to work through a fledgling sales and operations process. This included close working relationships with wholesalers, retail chains and bottle stores. We also helped general stores set themselves up for success, even if they were selling spirits for the first time.

The price point and co-promotion meant that consumers could buy a small bottle and a mixer to share with change to spare from a 5 kina note (approximately $AU5 in today's currency) – and it worked.

An integrated approach for your distillery business can work, too. Especially if you use a common language throughout.

Product development

The DISTIL process in my first book, *Still Magic: A gin distiller's guide for beginners,* provides a good starting point for product development. In short, it describes a process where you **decide** what to **investigate** and

sample, then **test** those ideas in a systematic fashion. After various **improvements** and business considerations, you can ready yourself to **launch** your product.

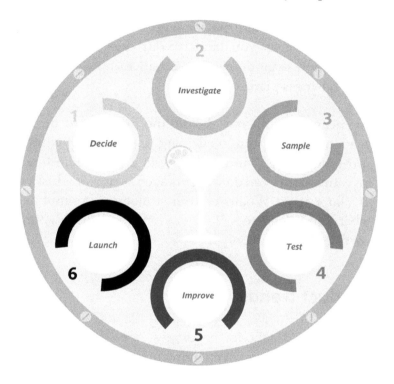

You can, of course, consider engaging a third party to assist your efforts. The choice is yours. There are advantages and disadvantages to either approach. Be sure to wear your time, cost and quality lenses to support your objective reasoning efforts.

Product selection

With so many spirit types available, I expect that you have already confirmed which product category you will pursue, but there may be several categories under consideration as you launch your quest for world domination over time – be certain to note these in your business plan.

For instance, you may devote the first one to three years of your venture on driving revenue from white spirits such as gin and vodka, with a view to finding investment for aged dark spirits such as rum or whisky at a later stage. Whatever your strategy is, commit to what you intend to sell on day one, and focus your energies there and only there.

Product trends

Trends in alcoholic beverages are dynamic as consumer tastes evolve. Innovators and incumbent producers need an understanding of the marketplace.

The international marketplace is far more accessible to producers now than it ever has been before, so tapping into product trends has never been easier. This is thanks to a combination of technology, social media and the rise of real-time connectedness that pervades our everyday lives. Interestingly, focus on adult beverages is increasingly aimed at moderate drinking, sociability, health, individual responsibility and responsibility as a good host.

Low alcohol/low sugar

Low alcohol, low sugar and quality packaging solutions for super-premium products are becoming more prevalent. In 1990s Australia, the earliest examples of low-alcohol brewed offerings manifested themselves as alcoholic sodas (Subzero[89]), alcoholic lemonade (Two Dogs[90]) and one of my favourite projects to deliver, alcoholic cola (XLR8[91]). In many ways, these products provided the blueprint for a twenty-first-century trend: the seltzer. Brands such as White Claw have become a global phenomenon with a focus on low-alcohol, low-sugar content and fresh crisp flavours in several different varieties. White Claw's packaging also demonstrates a sense of fun and vitality that resonates strongly with today's most adventurous consumer group, the Millennials (see 'The Generation Game' section).

Other examples of this approach include Pals from New Zealand[92] and Basic Babe from Australia.[93]

For many years, the 750 ml format was *de rigueur* for spirits packaging in Australia. This changed in the mid-1990s when United Distillers Australia (now Diageo) led the industry change to what is now the seemingly ubiquitous 700 ml (70cl) format used in the European Union (EU). In late 2020, the United States allowed importation of products in the 700 ml packaging size, thus removing a significant barrier to entry for all international spirits producers.[94]

According to a study from the IWSR, most markets are expecting to see a growth in no- and low-alcohol products.[95] Leading the way are South Africa, the United States and Spain. The next cohort includes the United Kingdom, Japan and Brazil, followed by Germany, France, Canada and Australia.

The driver behind this growth lies in perception changes. Low- or no-alcohol options are no longer perceived in a negative light. In fact, according to the IWSR, they are now considered aspirational.[96] Quite a marked change in attitude, I am sure you will agree.

This insight can potentially have impacts on your business plan. Is it worthwhile pursing the low-/ no-alcohol route? After all, no alcohol in the final product means no excise liability. It therefore becomes a financially attractive option to consider.

Before you decide, 'Hell yeah!' remember that, like every simple thing, it will likely not be easy. The technical challenges associated with producing high-quality, delicious low-alcohol adult beverages cannot be understated. Even commercial breweries, with a wealth of resources at their disposal, have taken a measured and cautious approach to this concept.

That said, your operation could well be the disruptor in a market that is growing in popularity. That's an aspiration worth raising a glass to at the least.

Subscription models

Once the retail mainstay of wine producers world-wide, subscription models are proving to be a boon for craft spirits enthusiasts around the world. The upside for the consumer is product variety delivered consistently at regular intervals, based upon the type of subscription. Producers can leverage the benefit of having a business-to-consumer (B2C) retail channel available to them via partnerships with intermediaries. They supply product to a third-party distributor. The product or products are then repacked to fulfil subscription demands.

Some subscription services support producers and consumers by including value-add items. These can be as varied as merchandise, tasting notes and premium mixers to complement the product.

CASE STUDY – SUGGESTGIN

SuggestGin, Discerning Gin Tasting Society, is a superb example of a fresh approach to value-add subscription services.[97] Launched in January 2021, SuggestGin is the collective effort of four ginthusiasts from Aotearoa: Chief Botanical Officer Fraser Buchanan, Russell O'Brien, Nikki Hommes and Sarah Williams. If a subscriber would like to purchase more of a particular product, bottles have a QR code available which the subscriber can scan to help expedite a sales order with the maker.

SuggestGin's value-add items include member-only website access, access to weekly live and recorded streaming sessions with the makers, serving preference advice and full colour notebooks with tasting tips, visual aids for sensory assessment and descriptions of the makers' own stories.

The care and attention SuggestGin gives to the three cash drivers – product, brand/marketing and distribution – brought together as an integrated whole is clear to see, from the provenance of the producers to the consumer's glass. This is a superb example of an excellent model to emulate; one that will bring low-cost value-add to your business, help you connect with your consumers and enhance your standing in the marketplace.

Canned cocktails

RTDs, alcopops and canned cocktails all present an opportunity for your business to consider as part of future product offering. This will be the key growth area for United States craft spirits in years to come.[98]

CASE STUDY – UNITED DISTILLERS LIMITED

My introduction to canned cocktails came via my role as a new product development specialist with United Distillers (Australia) Limited (UDL) in the 1990s. UDL is an Australian brand of pre-mixed adult beverage. In various parts of the world, these beverages are also known as a canned cocktails, alcopops or ready to drinks (RTDs). The UDL RTD name and brand in Australia first saw the light of day in 1965, in the Australian state of Victoria.[99]

UDL RTD products epitomised the casual, informal light-heartedness of the Australian way of life for decades. They reflected the times as well with UDL Vodka Lemon, Lime and Soda, UDL Rum and Cola, UDL Gin and Tonic, UDL Brandy, Lime and Soda, and UDL Ouzo and Cola. When the RTD market was still a fledgling segment in the adult beverage category, UDL was the first to offer this packaging format.

In the early 1990s, premiumisation began to take hold, with Bundaberg Distilling Company partnering with producers to create Bundaberg UP and Cola, Bundaberg OP and Cola (using underproof and overproof rum, respectively), and Dark 'n' Stormy, my first new product development project and joint venture assignment.

This was the first premium RTD produced in Australia in both cans and bottles. Johnnie Walker and Cola followed suit as a premium branded RTD in a frosted glass container.

In later years, generic RTDs began to appear in bottles, though cans were the predominant format. These in turn underwent a major update in 1999 with the onset of brands such as Lemon Ruski coming into play. Lemon Ruski's formula attracted less excise than RTDs of the same strength. This improved profit margin without compromising quality.

Product risks to manage

Making something – anything – is often the combination of three elements wrapped up in a little bundle of joy called risk (it turns up everywhere, so stay awake). The three elements of interest are time, cost and quality.

You may recall the '*If... then*' structure from earlier in the book. For simplicity, let's look at the risks of choosing any two of the three elements and ignoring the third as it is far easier to balance two things than three.

Here are some potential risks to consider in each case:

- *If* you focus on cost and time, *then* product quality is at risk and may not be fit for purpose.

- *If* you focus on time and quality, *then* product cost is at risk and may adversely impact finance.

- *If* you focus on quality and cost, *then* time to market is at risk and may adversely impact your ability to compete in a timely manner.

Risk is an active consideration in all your business dealings. Product risk in manufacturing is no different, regardless of your business size. Focus on risks for a small operation for now, knowing that the concepts are readily transferable to larger operations.

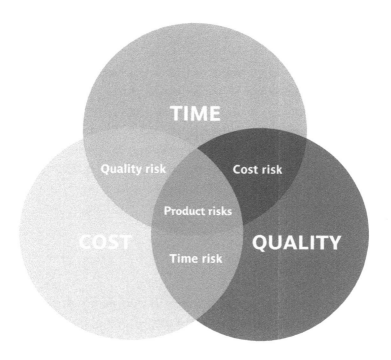

The risks to consider are numerous, ranging from poor quality dry goods to noncompliant labels, product recall, issues in assembly and mismatched packaging. I have seen a number of budding spirits businesses suffer when their bottle, closure and label selection did not integrate easily for release to market. Build in provisions to discuss challenges with people on the ground as part of the road trips we looked at earlier in the book.

You can often view risk as an opportunity to learn. Don't be afraid to reframe it this way.

Safety considerations

Product safety can make or break your business. Poor quality glass subject to breakages, foreign bodies in bottles, poorly fitting closures, insecure shippers, product breakages in supply, poor plant hygiene, poor plant housekeeping – any one of these factors can compromise good manufacturing practice and safe operation. Be aware of what could go wrong and figure out your response to manage the risk.

Summary

- You need a product strategy. If people are not particularly fussed about your offering, no matter how good it is, it will not sell.

- The good news is that craft spirits lie in a large, profitable and extremely popular product type.

- Will eCommerce or some other route be your favoured path to market?

- Make sure everyone on your production process is speaking the same language – sometimes quite literally!

- Use the DISTIL process in your product development.

- Look at product trends such as low-alcohol or low-sugar drinks.

- Consider RTDs, canned cocktails and alcopops as future offerings.

- Examine how time, cost and quality influence how you approach risk.

- View risk as an opportunity to learn.

- Visit other operations to understand and manage the multitude of risks your business will deal with.

9

Brand

A rguably the most important part of your business, brand is also the most intriguing. If brand were a chess piece, it would likely be a knight, complete with its unique movements: two steps forwards, backward, left or right followed by one taken at right-angles to the landing point. The ability to attack an adversary in a multitude of different ways. Similar movements can claim brand positions, either unoccupied or occupied, with equal aplomb.

What exactly is a brand, though? Is it really as readily definable as a chess piece?

In a business context, your brand communicates who you are, where you are from, what you do... you'll know the rest of the story from here, I'm sure. Brand is a serious business. Although the analogy above is tongue-in-cheek, it does show some legitimate dimensions to branding.

For people with an operations bent, the whole notion of branding, sales and marketing tends to be a baffling business black box. When your strength is in making things, the psychology associated with sales and marketing can also be a source of scepticism.

'Ha! This product can sell itself,' is a common catch cry in manufacturing facilities in startups. Listen up, folks. Like it or not, every business is a sales organisation at heart. Success is not built solely upon the products that the organisations sell. The brand story – the hero's journey – is key to enduring financial success.

For example, fast-food giant McDonald's does not make – nor claim to make – the best burgers in the market, but they're certainly the most popular.[100] Apple was the first trillion-dollar company on the planet, and its appeal lives on, despite some claiming the company doesn't make the best products anymore.[101] Jay Z does not produce the best hip-hop music on the planet, but he still became the genre's first billionaire.[102]

Trout and Ries's immutable marketing law states: 'It's better to be first than it is to be better.'[103]

Check out any episode of *The Apprentice UK*,[104] and you will see that notion writ large. In fact, I would strongly recommend you take in every episode of the latest series. It's a learning experience on so many different levels, where people's strengths and weaknesses ultimately give way to one thing: their ability or inability to sell.

The real point of interest for me lies in the diverse backgrounds the candidates come from: tax, information technology, acting, law, quality control, professional speaking, learning and development, tree surgery, sponsorship, sports events, eco cleaning, lifestyle branding (yes, products makers, it's a thing), vegan confectionary and swimwear. Yet the three finalists tend to have had one thing in common: good branding.

What is a brand?

A brand is someone's perception of a product, service, experience or company, often based on an identifying logo, name and presence. Brands can come and go depending upon individual perceptions in the marketplace. Those that endure offer something different; something that resonates strongly with specific individuals. This concept is one that craft spirits producers can use as an opportunity to stand out.

Creating a brand narrative that resonates with consumers and encourages people to buy is key. This book will not explore branding concepts in depth; there are many resources available to assist with this part of the business strategy, and I'm sure you product-making entrepreneurs want to get things going as soon as you can. Suffice to say branding is of huge importance. Branding sets the tone and direction of your business.

In many ways, a brand is the face of your enterprise. It represents your business ethos. It is also a two-edged sword as different customers will seek to access your brand via numerous media channels – social media in particular – so brand consistency is crucial.

When it comes to sharing your brand, don't be like a parent bombarding polite friends with photographs of every living moment shared with their child. Be selective about whom you intend to share it with. If people are turned off from the get-go, no amount of attractive product promotion and pricing will convince them to stay with you.

Ask yourself these questions:

- What is the story behind my business?
- Why should people buy my product?
- Is it like any other product?
- What sets my brand apart?

- What problems does it solve?

- Why is it so expensive?

- Why is it so cheap?

- Why should my ideal customer care?

- How do I express my product solution so folks say, 'Hell yeah' and not 'Meh'?

Think of the branding iron for cattle. It is a clear statement about identity and where each animal belongs in the herd, and so it is with your business brand. A brand is *not* just your product, name, logo, website or social media handle; it's a combination of these elements. In fact, it runs far deeper than that.

Brand strategy

Your brand strategy is whatever needs doing to ensure that individuals know what your business is about. It describes the ways and means that are different to other businesses to present your brand story to a specific market. It is unlikely that your story will be the same as anyone else's, so you immediately have an advantage.

Key inputs into your strategy include:

- What purpose do you (and your brand) serve?

- What sets you apart (your USP)?

- What business vision do you intend sharing?

- What will you do better than others doing the same thing?

- What values and cultural standards are important to you?

- What will you and your brand promise to deliver to your customers?

- How will you take your story and branding messages to market?

- What reputation do you want the market to ascribe to you?

These important questions need the best answers for your business, so it may be a case of getting expert help.

You also need to be crystal clear about who the individuals are that you want to get your message to. With a global population that is technologically connected in real-time, a scatter gun approach where you are trying to be all things to all people will not be anywhere near as effective as carefully targeting a select cohort (or niche) that your brand will interest.

Your ideal customer

If you were to put yourself into the shoes of the customer you really want your brand to attract, how would you describe them? What is it about them that you believe would resonate with your brand? What would a day in the life of your ideal customer look like?

These are simple questions, but answering them is not easy. It can be tempting to consider yourself as the ideal customer, but describing your customer as an extended version of yourself is a trap you need to avoid falling into. To mitigate this risk, I strongly recommend that you consider attending workshops and peer reviews with experts when you're building up this description. This will help to create buy-in within your team (if you have one at this stage) and reduce the likelihood of two common barriers to progress:

- Confirmation bias. This is where people favour information that confirms their belief and dismiss information that does not.

- Group think, where the urge to conform and not rock the boat leads to poor decision making that can put your business goals at risk.

The difficult exercise of deciding on your ideal customer can be made easier if you're clear about what that customer looks like. Perhaps create a digital representation – an avatar – using freely available software tools, or merely list their attributes.

What demographics does your customer fall into: gender, marital status, age-range, income? What are your ideal customer's job responsibilities: company director, middle manager, team leader, junior professional, university graduate, high school graduate, student? Where does your customer get their information from? What do they read? When do they read? What social media do they use?

Chances are, you will know people who seemingly fit the persona you are describing. When you have a clear persona for your ideal customer, apply the 'like' rule, finding an example among your social circles. You can then put a name and a face to the persona. For example, 'Like Aunt Mable, Cousin Margaret, Maddie's brother-in-law', or maybe 'More like Beyoncé than Lady Gaga.' Let your imagination run wild – but do the donkey work first. Finding the person, and then retrofitting their character / avatar to match may create more difficulties later.

The notion of an avatar is more widespread than you may think. There is likely a digital 'you' out there, based upon your online behaviour. Cookies are the key to constructing the ideal customers to target and are the lifeblood of digital marketing efforts across platforms.

Branding decisions

Your brand is shaped by your name, logo, website, blogging and posting voice on social media. It's the experience you want your ideal customers to enjoy, and the heartfelt emotions you have toward your business.

Yes, that's lots to think about, but it all starts with you, your story and the way you present it. It's this key component that will make your brand memorable.

In her book *Let's Get Visible!*,[105] author Sapna Pieroux describes a simple and effective way to consider all your branding decisions and the inevitable revisions that will take place: DoSaySee.

DoSaySee is an awareness framework that puts your brand at the centre of three intersecting circles. 'Do'

refers to the problem you are solving. 'Say' refers to how you will communicate your business messages to your ideal customer. 'See' refers to all the visible solutions to customer problems that bring your company to life.[106]

To build your brand, you must illustrate and/or describe what you do for others, what you say to them and what they see when you do what you say. In other words, how effectively are consumers understanding your messages?

When these three elements are aligned and in balance, then you have the basis to build a great brand that will solve a problem for your customer in ways they will readily understand.

But beware. The longer it takes to release a product, the more expensive it will be. From my experience, this concept has an equally nefarious twin: quick and cheap ultimately becomes slow and expensive. To understand the problem you are solving, you'll need to be clear on your ideal customer's demographics.

Branding basics for the twenty-first century

For most businesses this century, there are fundamental areas that form branding pillars. Branding strategy hasn't changed a lot in principle since my post-grad days at Edinburgh Business School, but the rate of change in the environment and real-time connectedness means that there are other market forces to contend with.

As a bare minimum – and in no particular order – you will need to apply some quality thinking to these areas:

Colours

Get the colours associated with your brand right, and it will go a long way.

> **EXERCISE: Colour schemes**
>
> Think of some brands that immediately come to mind when you consider certain colour schemes:
>
> - Light blue – Facebook, Twitter, LinkedIn
> - Red and yellow – McDonalds, Royal Dutch Shell
> - Green, white and yellow – British Petroleum (BP)
> - Red, black and white – Kentucky Fried Chicken (KFC)
> - Red, blue, yellow and green – Google

Website

With so many sites out there and people's attention spans getting shorter, the key is to maintain interest through simplicity once you have gained it.

To do this effectively, make sure:

- Your website is easy to understand and navigate
- The brand's logo transitions cleanly from page to page
- Typeface and colour palette are consistent (no mixed typefaces)

Your domain name can be as easy to get right as it is to get wrong. Here are a few tips to consider. Make sure your domain name is:

- Easy to remember
- Easy to spell; no funky bogan spellings
- Short
- Consistent with the brand and, importantly, your keywords

Time invested here is well spent.

Sometimes, your inspiration can come from the most unlikely sources. For example, my inspiration for the two-word book title *Still Magic* came from Muhammed Ali. In addition to being a three-time heavyweight boxing champion of the world, he had an amazing ability to create a poem.

He delivered a speech to a raft of newly capped Harvard graduates in the early seventies, receiving a rousing reception when someone asked him for a poem.[107] Silence fell as he rose from his seat, lifted his hands for quiet and uttered two words:

'Me...' while pointing to himself. 'We...' while extending his arms to the graduates. As uproarious applause broke out, the world's shortest speech came to a memorable conclusion.

If the greatest boxer of all time can say a lot with two words, how hard can it be? It took me about ten weeks to find a two-word answer; Ali took ten seconds to deliver an immortal two-word speech. Guess that is why *he* is the greatest of all time.

Logo

If there is a branding element that punches well above its weight, it is a well-thought-out and well-crafted logo. The most memorable logos are noted for their simplicity and elegance.

Examples of universally well-known logos are the Nike swoosh, McDonald's golden arches and the shell motif for Dutch Shell. In the spirits industry, there is Johnnie Walker's striding gentleman, the Gordon's Gin boar, the Bacardi bat, Bundaberg Rum's polar bear, Wild Turkey's epic poultry, the Four Roses bunch of flowers and the four dots representing the cornerstone values that support the Four Pillars narrative and brand name.

Simple. Elegant. Recognisable. Representative.

Tone of voice

A simple question that is notoriously hard to answer is: what does your brand 'sound' like? This is equally vital to consider in business to business (B2B) and B2C communications.

All messages and interactions, be they digital or real life, need mindful thought and consideration. Whatever your business 'voice' is, it needs to reflect:

- How you're expecting the brand to be perceived in the marketplace

- The platform you're using (formal such as email, informal such as social media) – in popular musical terms, think usual release versus extended dance mix

When you consider that branding is all about perceptions, tone of voice can be one of the most challenging aspects to tackle. You need to find your voice, expressing that to your ideal customer while retaining authenticity and consistency during periods of change and upheaval.

Let's go back to music as an analogy. How many times have you heard people refer to a band's old stuff being so much better than their new stuff? The best approach is to find your perfect voice for the here and now, then determine if this has the potential go into the future. Musicians and bands can undergo reinvention and changes to their line-ups, but they will need to seek out replacements who share the same tone of voice. This is also true of your brand.

CASE STUDY – G&J GREENALL

A superb example of how changes in line-up have managed to keep a narrative consistent, relevant and vibrant is G&J Greenall.[108]

Thomas Dakin, the forefather of quality English gin, purchased a property in Bridge Street, Warrington. He began distilling his original gin in 1761 at the age of twenty-five, and founded what would become the oldest gin distillery in England.

Joanne Moore is the master distiller for this operation and has held the post for over twenty years. In the 250 years that have elapsed since Thomas Dakin started the operation, there have been a total of seven master distillers, including Joanne.

That's right, a mere seven in 250 years.

You need to consider 250 years of history in your own part of the world to appreciate this brand's resilience. Having stood the test of time through monarchical changes, global human conflict, global pandemics, changes in geo-political landscapes, societal changes, changes in technology and the rise of social media, an eighteenth-century brand still more than holds its own in a twenty-first-century world of high-paced change and real-time connectedness.

Image

All images need to tie the previous points together. It's that simple, but not easy. Colours, logo, website all need to reflect the brand's tone in a consistent, memorable fashion so that your visual statement is as effective as every other statement you make.

Now that you've got all these elements lined up, the essential consideration is consistency. The term is many splendoured, but from a brand viewpoint, it boils down to what your customers experience today looking pretty much the same as yesterday, so they can confidently expect more of the same tomorrow.

Consistency is a difficult concept to execute, but crucial in all media, be it:

- Emails – the greeting, close and signature block

- Blogs – content, language and structure

- Social media – content and image size limits differ between platforms

- Hashtags – some platforms such as LinkedIn penalise overuse

Many of the elements described in this section may be thought of as 'mastering the mundane' – a regular, consistent approach to addressing the little things. This may not be particularly exciting, sexy, ground-breaking or epic, but it's crucial to your brand.

Anyone who exercises regularly will know that warming up and warming down are not the high-lights of their workout. No one ever sets a personal best for stretching, but exercising without these bookend routines can cause injury, leading in turn to time when people can't exercise and the resultant frustration. Treat the little things in your branding in a consistent, measured way, just like a fitness warm up campaign, progressing and strengthening your brand as you go. It doesn't get easier; you merely become stronger and develop greater capacity.

Here are some branding ideas to glean from the field:

- Post creative and market-specific content (Pabst Blue Ribbon)[109]

- Make your visual content cohesive with a good theme (Smirnoff)[110]

- Converse with fans and humanise your business (Dogfish Head)[111]

- Present a lifestyle your market can relate to (Bacardi)[112]

- Use images and videos whenever possible (Jim Beam)[113]

- Keep your content current and don't sell too aggressively (Dos Equis)[114]

- Cross-promote with social media takeovers[115]

Naming your enterprise

Ignore any inclination you may have to describe your new business as your 'baby'. This does a disservice to babies worldwide. Naming processes for a baby and a craft spirits business are not the same thing. Not even close.

With that off my chest, here are some great ways to brainstorm a company or brand name that you can rightfully call your own, along with everyday examples:

- A functional promise – No More Nails

- Catchy phrase – Dark 'n' Stormy, Still Magic

- Create a word, acronym or initials based on the creators' names – ABBA (Agnetha, Björn, Benny, Anni-Frid), Will.i.am, LVMH (Louis Vuitton Moët Hennessy)

- Initials based on the function of the product – VHS (Video Home System)

- Use a creator's name – Brogan's Way, Reed and Co, Freeland Spirits, Jack Daniels, George Dickel, Thomas Daikin, Uncle Nearest

- A life experience – Broken Heart Spirits, Finders, Flowstate

- Use a location – Islay, Skye, Bundaberg, Edinburgh, Manly, Coromandel

- Use a term expressing your heritage and intent – Karu (Estonian for bear)[116]

- Leverage names and interests – Poor Toms

- Words from other languages – Audi (the Latin translation of the German founder's surname – Horch – meaning to hark or listen)

- Alliteration – Never Never, GinGin

Test-driving the name

As much as you may love a name dripping with wittiness, personality and derring-do, it has a functional purpose. It needs to be attention grabbing, easy to say and easy to remember. This becomes even more vital when you receive phone calls, register trademarks and seek domain names for websites.

Good stress tests to apply are:

- Brevity – Cardhu, Hendrick's, Gordon's

- One word with three to four syllables – Rentokil, Aviation

- Two words totalling three to five syllables – Johnnie Walker, Four Pillars Gin, Freeland Spirits, Pinckney Bend, Burger King

CASE STUDY – ROGUE SOCIETY

Two brothers-in-law and a musician spent time together, discussing how they had always wanted to make their own gin – so they did. Twelve botanicals, water from the rugged Southern Alps, an old still in a shed – all the makings of a great story.

International gold-medal winning accolades followed, in London and San Francisco. Given their international success, it would have made perfect sense for the founders to stock their gin in these places. That is where the Rogue Society team really did make a name for themselves in the most unexpected way.[117]

To their joy and delight, representatives from the EU expressed interest in stocking their gin for sale. All was good in the world and opportunity beckoned.

Then one day, they struck difficulties. Unless you are a trademark lawyer, it is difficult to understand why a market cannot have two products in different alcohol categories – in this case, beer and spirits – with similar looking names. The intent is to limit the risk of a visitor to the EU using a brand name to order one thing there and receiving something different, It just so happened that Rogue was associated with a beer in the United States. The simplest solution would have been to insist that the American brewing behemoth change their name so that the Rogue Society producers could sell their gin in the EU. How hard could it be?

In short, the brewer did not want to change its name, so Rogue Society quite literally made a name for itself in more ways than one. Rogue Society Gin is now known as Scapegrace, a little-used eighteenth-century English synonym for a rogue. All is right in the world once again.

Branding risks to manage

If what you customers see and hear you say does not match what you do, *then* your message will come across as insincere and difficult to trust. *If* what you do and what your customers see does not match what you say, *then* you will be incoherent and hard to understand. *If* what you do and say does not match what your customers see, *then* you will be invisible to them in the crowd.

CASE STUDY – SOUTHWEST AIRLINES

Founded in 1967 by Herbert Kelleher and Rollin King, Southwest Airlines sought to 'democratise the skies'.[118] The idea was that if Kelleher and King could do this better than anyone else, and do it profitably, then they would be on to a winner.

This premise was based on following three operating principles:

- Low prices to attract mass market appeal
- The friendliest culture in the industry
- Outstanding customer experiences

Low prices meant cutting OpEx, one of the challenges that all distilleries need to consider at all stages. Kelleher and King did this by using only one type of aircraft, the knock-on being that pilot and flight-attendant training was simplified and less expensive than training for a variety of different aircraft.

Southwest hired people who delivered superb customer service to every customer every time, from start to finish. The first check-in bag would be free, the second bag free, flight changes free, reserving seats free, snacks and drinks free. The branding had, and still has, a wholesome feel-good vibe to it.

To date, Southwest Airlines has generated $US20 billion in revenue, has nearly 58,000 employees and was voted most-loved United States airline in 2019.

Southwest lessons for your distillery:

- Use standard packaging components when branding. One bottle type, one label type, size and design format, one closure, one sealing method, one shipper (carton) to accelerate speed to market for additional products. This will ease the training burden when you grow and need people to help out.

- Take calls from customers with a smile in your voice. You have one chance to make a good first impression with your story. They have lots of chances to ruin it for you. Everyone knows the tale of *that* one bad TripAdvisor, Yelp or Google review.

• Have a culture that puts your customer and their experiences at the centre of attention. Your site tours and the sense of openness they engender will provide a great opportunity to do just that.

Social media

Social media can be a minefield, so it's worthwhile expanding upon this a little more, given that it is the playground for the technologically savvy consumer. The various platforms, such as Instagram and LinkedIn, change their engagement algorithms on a regular basis. Quality content will always get the job done better than investing time to outsmart a tech platform and its algorithm.

Social media is huge and largely unregulated, meaning that young people can view and engage with content that may not be suitable for them. This includes alcohol advertising, which is doubly challenging when the big alcohol companies are investing vast sums of money into it. To put this into context, on average, people will scroll through 96 m (nearly 300 feet in imperial measurement) of content on any given day.[119] That's the length of an American football field.

This is further complicated by the prevalence of young adult 'influencers' receiving approaches to endorse products and offers of lucrative compensation for doing so. The issue becomes even more cloudy when one considers the large number of underage followers that powerful influencers have in their squads.

Presenting an underage follower with a choice to make regarding alcohol, based upon endorsement from an influencer, is a sticky situation for your brand to be in – but what can you do?

One thing is to pressure (influence, if you will) the social media platforms to lift their game and invest time in minimising the risk of underage followers being exposed to alcohol endorsement. At the time of writing, Instagram has stated that it will introduce age-restricted posts in future. The knock-on effect of this, of course, is that the platform will receive less revenue, influencers will likely receive less compensation and the alcohol companies will have a different problem to solve.

What does that mean for you, as an entrepreneur? In short, be selective about how you use your social media channels, choose your influencers carefully and be aware that underage folks may view your content.

Now that you have seen the digital problem that exists today, how would this look in an analogue/

non-digital world? What steps can you take to minimise the impacts of your product upon underage
people in the 'real world' and how do you address a
complaint should one arise?

The 2020 Australian Distilled Spirits Association
conference had a superb presentation from former
Commonwealth of Australia Attorney General,
Michael Lavarch, representing The Australian Beverages Alcohol Code (ABAC).[120] The equivalent of this
organisation in the United Kingdom is the Portman
Group,[121] and it's the TTB Alcohol Beverage Advertising in the United States.[122]

The key takeaways from this presentation were for
alcohol producers to make sure they understand:

- Consumer and competition law

- The advertising code of ethics

- Responsible alcohol marketing codes

- State liquor licencing

- Specific codes for television and outdoor venues

The core standards to consider are:

- Responsible and moderate portrayal of alcohol

- Responsibility toward minors in terms of content
  and placement

- Responsible depiction of alcohol effects
- Alcohol and safety

If by any chance a customer raises a complaint, in Australia, this process will take place:

- Complaint lodged with advertising standards
- Advertising standards refers all complaints to ABAC
- If the complainant has raised an ABAC issue, the producer receives an invitation to respond to the complaint
- ABAC panel addresses the complaint and the response
- Complaint upheld or dismissed
- If the complaint is upheld, then removal or modification of the offending brand is sought

Trying to administer compliance of any description across a single geography is no mean feat. A backdrop of real-time connectedness and perhaps several geographies merely escalates the challenge. The bottom line is to consider your branding narrative in its entirety. Maintain diligence concerning how your images (including packaging, label design, motifs, animations, typefaces), voice/tone, logo, website and other branding components may generate unwanted attention.

That said, do not let these considerations dominate your creative planning and thinking. A little considered risk management early in the process will save a significant amount of fan cleaning later.

The Generation Game

Social commentators often posit that consumer behaviour differs between generations of people. Further, there are 'era definitions', albeit somewhat arbitrary in nature, that they use to ascribe neat timeframes to behavioural bundles. As you build your business plan with expert help and a view to pitching your distillery idea to others, chances are you'll be dealing with people that span as many as five generations.

I have summarised the keys in the following table, so you can garner input and support for your business and present it in ways that resonate with your audience.

Craft spirits makers need to consider their consumers' wants and needs, regardless of the generation that they occupy. They also need to consider how best to lead intergenerational teams. This is a two-edged sword.

Generation	Era	Mantra	How to lead/what they look for
Builders	1933–1945	Be grateful you have a job	• Ask questions with genuine interest and active listening
Baby Boomers	1946–1964	I deserve better	• Teamwork • Crusading a cause • Data and process • Status rewards
Generation X (Gen X)	1965–1981	Keep it real	• Work-life balance • Role significance • Offer independence • Reward by recognition on merit
Millennials (Gen Y)	1982–1999	Life is a buffet	• Mentor/coach; do not command • Transparent leadership, fun, stability • Meaningful work • Reward with learning opportunities
Generation Z (Gen Z)	1996–2011	I'm coping and hoping	• Brief, frequent feedback • Clear direction • Pictures • Flexibility to work independently • Offer opportunities to fast-track advancement • Reward with recognition and chances for personal growth

For instance, Millennials – the most avid consumers of craft spirits on the planet[123] – may believe that they understand their own generation better than most and look inwardly as being the best at representing their interests. What happens, though, if you are not a Millennial, yet need to present a message geared toward resonating with them? This was precisely the challenge that a classic product line from Diageo – Johnnie Walker – took head on, which forms the basis for a case study in the next chapter, 'Marketing'.

Branding plays a significant part in your business before, while and after you make the first of your many sales. It concerns perceptions at every level, personal, product and business, and is one of the most important factors in your business success. This section barely touched the surface. It has, however, provided a level of awareness and, to some extent, a minimum level of investment as you build your business and its brand.

There are some aspects of branding which are downright concerning, some that are bewildering and some that are wickedly exciting and fun. Approach every area of your branding strategy with enthusiasm and gusto, getting help in the areas that you believe will be a struggle before you reach them.

Be prepared for the long haul. The ups and downs will be numerous, the problems to solve will be endless and demanding, but if you have a resilient sense of purpose, they won't stop you from creating a great brand.

Summary

- Branding sets the tone and direction of your business.

- A brand is someone's perception of a product, service, experience or company, often based on an identifying logo, name and presence.

- In many ways, your brand is the face of your enterprise. It represents your business ethos.

- Consistency is crucial as different customers seek to access your brand via numerous media channels.

- You are far more likely to stand out if you target specific individuals, your ideal customer, rather than trying to be all things to all people.

- Be clear on what problem you are solving for your ideal customer. It must be one they will readily understand.

- The longer it takes to release a product, the more expensive it will be, but equally, quick and cheap ultimately becomes slow and expensive.

- The branding elements to consider include colours, logo, tone of voice and image.

- Consider the advice we've looked at in this chapter when choosing your brand name.

- Make sure all messaging related to you brand is consistent. Remember DoSaySee – if your customers don't see and experience what you say you're going to do, they will receive mixed messages and likely look to your competitors.

- Bear in mind the ways in which the different generations receive messages and what resonates with each one.

- How will you mitigate the risk of underage followers being exposed to your brand by advertisers and influencers?

10
Marketing

There are few more terrifying, ambiguous or hazardous expeditions for a spirits maker to take than a trip down Marketing Lane. The Marketing Module in my post-graduate studies was the largest, most detailed and arduous tome I've ever had to take on. Like it or not, marketing needs time, effort and attention from someone with the capacity to do it justice.

You may be the right person in the right seat to do the right thing with marketing. Or you may not be and will have to learn all you can about it. It is hard, no doubt about it. Finding ways to convince customers to take a call to action that is profitable to you and meaningful to them is tough.

You require a combination of strategy and tactics to position your products in the marketplace in ways that motivate people to buy. For me, as a marketer, I recognise my limitations, and they comprise the mere basics to get started in marketing.

In my case, and possibly in yours, too, getting expert help is the best option for everyone concerned.

Marketing fundamentals

If you don't get expert help now, unless you are a marketing expert yourself, you will pay the price sooner or later. 'Sooner' means that you will take on this challenge, likely having to learn from the ground up and consume a lot of time and energy in so doing. A better use of time would be learning, reading and conversing with experts. 'Later' means that you may have taken up the challenge, but not necessarily seen the outcome or consequences – good or bad – resulting from decisions you took sooner.

> **PRO TIP**
>
> If in any doubt, plan to get expert help for your marketing. Move slowly away from the scene so that no one gets hurt.

The overarching advice concerning marketing, then, is get expert help, but you can give yourself a grounding in the subject first. Here are some marketing fundamentals that will set the tone for your business.

Marketing your name

What is in a name? As you know from the 'Brand' chapter (Chapter 9), it's pretty much everything. Your business name is a key asset and will set the tone from day one. In that respect, it's no different to the name bestowed upon you at birth. It is yours and, interestingly, something you do not use nearly as much as other people do. Changing the name of your business, just like your given name, is no mean feat, so best invest some quality thinking into it up front.

Here are a few things to consider. Is your business name one you can take to market? Many people may share your given name, but this does not work well for the name of your business. Do as much research as you can to confirm that you can use your intended business name. Remember the case study in the previous chapter where Rogue Society was forced to change its name?

Registrations

Registering your name is key to marketing as well, so get on to this as soon as possible. The registrations cover:

- Company name

- Trading name

- Website domain name

- Email internet service provider (ISP) and hosting name

- Facebook page name

- Instagram page name

- Twitter account names

Time spent on getting your design right is time well spent. Why? Because it is an investment in your future – a future that at best is unclear, yet readily describable.

There are lots of resources available from online providers such as Upwork[124] or Fiverr[125] that can quickly and inexpensively bring your designs to life. That said, if you can afford to invest in well-credentialed professional services that have a track record with helping distilleries, then I recommend you do this. A great example of a professional outfit geared toward the branding and labelling requirements for a craft spirits operation is Stranger and Stranger in the United Kingdom.[126]

Marketing trends

As we saw in the previous chapter, Millennials are the most avid adopters of craft spirits globally. This is great news for producers and marketers alike. It also brings the importance of branding into focus, both for new and established operations.

When you have an established brand, pitching it to a new cohort of consumers is no mean feat. A strategy that targets a new market segment with a long-standing product is an expensive, resource-intensive exercise. When resources are scarce, this can signal a death knell before you make a genuine start.

CASE STUDY – JOHNNIE WALKER AND MILLENNIALS

Johnnie Walker is one of the world's most enduring whisky brands. The signature walking gentleman and the use of red and gold colouring makes the Johnnie Walker Red Label one of the most recognisable brands on the planet. However, it presented an image and acceptance challenge for a generation of drinkers: Millennials.

The challenge for Diageo, the owner of the Johnnie Walker brand and its suite of products, was to repackage its traditional story, steeped in Scottish history and values, then translate this into a contemporary expression that would appeal to the fastest-growing group of consumers in the world.[127]

Collaboration is regarded as the Millennials' secret sauce, so the advertisement's storyline concerns two Millennials struggling to make a dent in their chosen side-hustles: painting canvases and working in fashion.[128] They meet, exchange ideas and the results are fabrics bearing the canvas designs. They then celebrate their success with a Johnnie Walker product in a bar. All this for a cool £15m.[129]

Change takes courage and conviction. Here are some insights for reference:[130]

- Changing a time-honoured image, in Johnnie Walker's case retiring the famous walking gentleman. This is like dropping Colonel Sanders from KFC: a huge paradigm shift. However, there was recognition that the brand needed to adapt to changing times.

- Developing specialist campaigns for specific areas. Think about where you're selling and use approaches that are fit for purpose in that setting (eg tastings in off-premises settings).

- Trust, quality, premium branding. Trust and quality are key. Connect with your customers and your followers. Turn up to play all day, every day, consistently. Consistency is tough; the rewards will come, though. Trust is earned.

- Collaborations with likeminded value-led groups. There may well be groups or social causes that align with the values that you intend to use as a guide in your business. For instance, Johnnie Walker partnered with Uber, a clear message showing that consumers had a safe way home and that hosts had peace of mind.

Listen up, folks. Before you make a hash of your golden opportunity, take missteps with your marketing and bypass a certain market, ask whether you might be wiser to build your strategy around it. Remember, quick and dirty at the start ends up being slow and expensive; give your marketing strategy the respect it demands.

The good news is that startups generally have a clear vision of whom they are targeting with no plans to change strategy anytime soon.

Social media 7-11-4

When it comes to social media planning, scheduling and resourcing, this set of numbers is worth its weight in gold.

Google researchers determined that a customer requires seven hours of interaction across eleven touchpoints in four separate locations before they will make a purchase.[131] This concept is precisely what you can use to supercharge your marketing efforts to produce the right things for the right people at the right times using the right platforms.

The four moments of truth (MOTs) – there were three until Google popped with a zeroth moment of truth (ZMOT) – are:[132]

- ZMOT – online research

- First moment of truth (FMOT) – first exposure to the product

- Second moment of truth (SMOT) – purchase

- Third moment of truth (TMOT) – reaction and feedback

And then there is the actual moment of truth (AMOT), a term coined by Anit Sharma.[133] This describes the state of mind the consumer experiences between confirming an online order and receiving the goods or services.

Think about how you felt after a recent online purchase – maybe it was the 50% deposit on a copper still, or something more modest. Was it elation, dread or something in between?

Some of the concepts that you will need to consider in your social media marketing campaign are:

- Create assets that will help your customers buy from your business

- Seven hours of contact includes, but is not limited to:
  - Face-to-face interactions: bar takeovers, pop-ups or festivals
  - Working lunches: virtual tastings or team-building exercises
  - Developing a subscription model with value-add content from makers

- Digital media – videos, demos, podcasts, white papers, blogs, written testimonials

- Eleven touchpoints concerns any material people can use to learn more about you:
  - Brochures, email campaigns, newsletters, office shop, website, social media
  - Networking events, third-party website or review

- Four locations refer to your content marketing strategy:
  - Repurposing content for different audiences (eg Instagram, Facebook, LinkedIn, Twitter)
  - Writing blogs or content for influential websites
  - Asking customers for Google reviews

Creating communities with digital marketing

Matt Thomas has a simple, understandable approach that drives his C-Skool business.[134] This helps people focus on the right marketing activities.

Successful marketing in a digital space requires you to create community, just like in real life. This helps attract everyday people to your business based on common interests and a sense of purpose.

The key two-pronged question to pose is this: 'Who are you and what do you want?' Getting this clear in your own mind will free your thinking to address:

- How to connect with your audience

- How to create impact and influence

- How to convert interested people into consumers

The advantages of digital marketing in social media are manifold, but the intent is to:

- Reach more people

- Create a bigger impact

- Make more money

The key concept that sets Matt's strategy apart, and one that can help influence your own strategies, is that true connection does *not* start by creating content; it starts by expressing clarity about:

- Who you are

- What you want

- What you are here to do

- Who your prospects are

An equilateral triangle is formed between 'You' (as your brand), 'Work' (your product or service offering) and 'Them' (your audience and prospects).

When you have built a community, the steps that an engaged prospect will experience are 'know' (what they've seen), 'like' (what they've heard) and 'trust' (how they've been helped). Finally, the content itself needs to be consistent, on-brand, targeted and strategic.

Suffice to say, there is a lot to get a handle on. By all means, invest time into understanding how this all hangs together, but ultimately, your goal ought to be to find someone to delegate this to, so look to engage experts to make life easier for you. Consistency beats intensity hands down.

Why make business harder than it already is?

CASE STUDY – SOCIAL MEDIA IN PNG (THE WANTOK SYSTEM)

PNG, 1996: a time before the internet phenomenon really ramped up. Few people had the resources available to access it, anyway; 28.8kps dial-up was the bomb at the time, as was an extremely practical and reliable analogue mobile network. But nothing outdid the wantok system for communication speed.

A wantok is an important member of your social circle, family, tribe, clan, squad. They're someone with whom you share everything. PNG is the home to no fewer than 850 languages, accounting for one in every three languages spoken on the planet, so literacy, in a Western sense, is 'limited' to a father's language, a mother's language and a local language, usually Tok Pisin and English. This made communication challenging at the best of times, but a picture paints a thousand words. Bright colours and simple logos were the key to communication ease.

This meant that people could communicate message intent in their own languages with likeminded people. It was this system of communications – the wantok system – that drove word-of-mouth campaigns more effectively that anything I had ever seen. People would share messages with their wantok, who would then share them with their wantok, who likely spoke no fewer than four different languages. Sometimes the messages got confused and misinterpreted, but people leading purchasing decisions by example when translation fell flat more than made up for it. It was the most effective marketing asset available.

It was my first exposure to something akin to the juggernaut that has become social media and viral advertising. Simple messages, repeatedly shared and reinforced.

Social media platforms

If you are anything like me, you'll find the morass of social media platforms like trying to make yourself known in a big crowd of strangers. The 'usual' four platforms, if such a concept exists, are Facebook, Instagram, LinkedIn and Twitter. Each of these has technical nuances and different audiences.

Sharing an Instagram post uses an additional app and process (Regram). This makes it vastly different to Facebook or LinkedIn, where sharing is available natively. There are different character limits for messages that you intend to post, and posting pictures differs, too. For example, it is far more difficult to attach a picture to a post in LinkedIn than it is in Facebook or Instagram.

In short, it's a little like driving your car through Europe. The functions of the car are much the same wherever you go, but there are specific road rules that differ in each country. Knowing what all these differences are is akin to being technically multilingual.

The chances are you will have a favourite platform that meets your needs, and that is fine. Choose two platforms and focus on getting posts and quality content on them. Then as soon as you can, consider adding platforms to your social media campaigns. Bear in mind the incremental overhead associated with this; it's an important consideration. Creating the content is a vital (blue) activity that warrants your time. Posting your content is a functional (red) activity, so think about how you can delegate or outsource this as part of your business plan.

Marketing risks to manage

The major marketing risks that any operation needs to manage are shown in the table. In fairness, there is nothing onerous or burdensome about these. In fact, they are sensible and practical measures to consider.

Key standard	Example of a breach against the standard
The responsible and moderate portrayal of alcohol	Running a campaign condoning intoxication or drunkenness
Responsibility toward minors (both in content and placement of marketing)	A TV campaign – say a thirty-second advert – at times when children are watching
Responsible depiction of the effects of alcohol	Implying in a campaign that consuming alcohol is the key to success in life
Alcohol and safety	Showing people drinking, and then taking on an activity requiring heightened co-ordination such as driving, operating plant machinery or swimming

This list applies to craft spirits operations of any scale, and as such requires diligence and attention from the outset. ABAC in Australia offers an assurance service for distillers to pre-vet their marketing strategies prior to release;[135] an excellent risk-management approach. ABAC also has a document entitled 'Best Practice for Responsible Digital Alcohol Marketing',[136] which I would urge all distillers anywhere in the world to review and consider for future reference.

Safety considerations

Few makers consider safety in a marketing context. Safety here is aligned to a sense of wellbeing with implications for physical, mental, emotional and relationship health.

Products or product messages that portray viewpoints or activities which may put people's wellbeing at risk are an absolute no-go zone. This becomes even more important when you're considering young and vulnerable people. Is there any risk of them misinterpreting the messages that they see, hear and read in relation to your products?

Bear in mind that there are advertising laws that set the minimum age for actors and actresses in alcohol advertising. You should check for actor eligibility before investing time and effort into production.

Best remove the risk in the first place. Fan cleaning – you get the idea?

Summary

- If you don't feel you are the right person to head your marketing, be sure to get expert help.

- Your business name is a key asset that will set the tone from day one, so make sure you choose one you can take to market.

- Make sure you register all the names that need registering.

- Use online resources to bring your marketing designs to life.

- Consider trends in marketing, even if it means reinventing your signature products to appeal to new consumers.

- Take Google's 7–11–4 rule of digital marketing into account.

- Consider the four purchasing moments of truth for your customers.

- Create digital communities for your business to attract customers.

- Choose the social media platforms you want to concentrate on.

- Look at the marketing risks and how to manage them.

- Always keep consumer safety front of mind in your marketing campaigns.

11
Distribution

If there is one cash driver that needs love and attention right from the start, it is distribution. In fact, it needs to be a factor in all product, branding and marketing decisions. The only reason it is the last cash driver covered in the book is because operationally, it is one of the last things to execute to support product sales.

Making a great product, building a great brand and marketing the offering safely and effectively to your intended audience is all well and good, but unless you have a way of getting your pride and joy to consumers, you will be stuck with stock and nowhere to send it. A distribution strategy is a crucial investment in your product's viability and reach to consumers.

Distribution strategy

What is distribution? It encompasses several dimensions that help you determine which approaches best suit your needs over time. In simple terms, it's a vital specialist service that safely delivers your product to the end consumer at a competitive price.

The minefield of pricing

You have a product that you are justifiably proud to call your own. You have a small but enthusiastic band of supporters who love what you do, love what you make and the personalised service you provide with every bottle. You are making good money, too, especially while you and you alone are getting things done, but the key concept that often gets 'lost' with product distribution is pricing. This links to profit, and therefore business viability.

At some point, you will need third parties to help you grow your business. Growth is directly attributable to sales, and there are only so many sales a single person can cover on any given day. You need to seek help, essentially delegating the customer supply part of the sales equation to people with the experience, know-how and resources that you don't have at scale.

Of course, these services come at a cost that needs funding from your margin, so set your prices as if you have third parties helping you out already. Include distribution approaches in your business plan, covering a thoughtful strategy concerning payment terms, customer service, branding, marketing and communications.

Do it yourself (DIY) distribution

DIY distribution is the best way to get product to market for an operation that is in its early stages. As we've just seen, however, pricing is a key determinant for business viability, so *before* your product demand increases, you need to think about price margins for wholesalers and distributors. When determining your price structure, consider a scenario that has you working with other parties right now. What would that look like?

Visualising what the future will look like is a useful exercise to consider, especially when you find yourself delivering single bottles to bars or restaurants in the pouring rain. Surely you can delegate this to someone else, a specialist, when demand increases?

Here are the upsides of DIY distribution:

- High margins – you retain the margin in full.
- Personalised service – customers love this.

The best place to start is with your friends and family, and in your local area to get the community on board.

When you're doing it all yourself, you can create your own terms as well. Like a boss.

Here are the downsides of DIY distribution:

- Lack of resources – you are it, getting out there, getting it done.

- Managing receivables yourself – in other words, collecting money from customers.

- Customer management – as you get more customers on board, the high level of personal service may decline and you may lose focus.

- Burnout – this is a common outcome in new distillery operations as the sense of overwhelm and time pressures collide.

- Time is precious – your focus needs to be on blue work to drive business growth and finding people that can help you do this.

- Lost connections – when you're trying to do everything for everyone everywhere, it can be easy to lose sight of the community and connections you've made. Your ear to the ground – an important source of information concerning your customers – may be compromised due to a reduction in bandwidth. Again, it's a case of deciding to whom you can delegate red activities, to support your increasing range and scope.

- High logistics costs – every hour of every day spent fulfilling orders is an hour to fund, and delivery costs are high. This is doubly so if your operation is located in a rural or remote area.

Distribution can be as simple as walking to bars and clubs to make deliveries, or filling your backpack, attending a festival and selling your wares to walk-in traffic. Or it can be as sophisticated as managing sales orders against stock that is available to promise, managing backorders and organising third parties to deliver on your behalf.

Distribution channels

A distribution strategy needs to consider seven fundamental channels broken up into three groups. The rationale for the groupings considers market proximity, current production capacity and resource requirements.

Domestic channels the owner can manage:

- Cellar door / distillery site

- Online / eCommerce

- Off-premises retailers such as bottle shops, mixed businesses, supermarket chains

Domestic channels that need additional resources to manage:

- Liquor chains

- Wholesalers

- Distributors

International channels requiring specialist help to manage:

- Export

- Duty free, also known as global travel retail (GTR)

A risk can also be an opportunity. For instance, if a product goes gangbusters, your strategy needs to consider the risk of stock running out and managing backorder supply with your distribution partners.

You may be just starting out, but it is worthwhile considering what you need in place to support an export market a few years downstream. If a duty-free opportunity becomes available, many offerings are in 1-litre format, or multiple bottles in smaller volumes. Consider smaller product sizes – say 200 ml – as single, double or triple packs. This means devoting time to work out the COGS for these smaller formats. They are labour intensive to fill, awkward to label and close, and need outstanding high-quality packaging formats.

Channel	Pros	Cons	Risks to manage
Cellar door/ Factory	• Retain full profit margin	• Limited to site visitors	• Space in your location • Increase in manufacturing overhead
Online store	• Retain most margin	• Website creation and maintenance • Manual deliveries to customers • COGS • Orders arrive at any time • Shipping costs can be expensive to absorb • Packaging for bottle quantities can be expensive	• Large stockholding required • Site uptime • Missed orders • Running out of stock to supply customers

Continued

Cont.

Channel	Pros	Cons	Risks to manage
Wholesalers	• Greater reach to niche customers such as bars and restaurants	• Impact on margin with 12% discount • Chasing debtors • Customer management	• Your product is one of many • Attention to your product needs will undergo prioritisation
Retail chains	• Greater reach • Provide most of the services described in the American Production and Inventory Control Society definition of distribution[148] • Larger orders, reduced freight cost • National coverage • One single point of contact for payment	• Behemoths make the rules • Will impact margins so volume is key. Budget for 22% discount • The bigger organisations are, the more slowly they pay • Chain will dictate where and which stores will stock product • Excise payments due in the same month as the order	• Your business may not have the capacity to deliver large minimum orders (pallet lots in the main) • Late deliveries may result in sanctions • Shipping to stores instead of distribution centres requires a network servicing approach when resources are scarce

Channel	Pros	Cons	Risks to manage
Distributors	• Greater reach • Provide most of the services described in the American Production and Inventory Control Society definition	• Budget for 25% discount • Some insist upon excise paid upfront prior to delivery • Rarely national	• Cost for supplying samples and marketing collateral • Consider distributors with bond stores – bond stores allow you to move stock without the need to pay excise tax when it leaves your business location • One single point of contact for orders and order payments

The services the American Production and Inventory Control Society suggests you may reasonably expect third parties to provide to support your strategy are:

- Transportation

- Warehousing

- Inventory control

- Material handling

- Order administration

- Site and location analysis

- Industrial packaging

- Data processing

- Communications network for effective management

- Physical distribution and returning goods to the manufacturer

Armed with this list, you can confidently research your options and figure out which services are the right ones for you right now.

What is a wholesaler?

Wholesalers are entities that meet all the distribution activities listed above for thousands of different products. They are sometimes referred to as 'box movers', a term that understates the value they can bring to your business when you are seeking greater reach and the assistance to do so.

Some of the wholesalers' advantages lie in the resources and specialists available to them who can manage:

- Warehousing – taking guardianship of your pride and joy.

- Logistics – shipping your goods from A to B safely and efficiently with minimal fuss.

- Customer order consolidation – your products can 'hitch a ride' with others heading to the same customer destination; it's a bit like a one-stop shop for your customers.

- Debt collection – there's no romance without finance, so having a safe pair of hands available to collect your hard-earned cash is a tremendous asset.

- Customer management – they can handle order processing, back orders, returns and some of those other niggly time-consuming service elements that influence the overall customer experience. You want customers coming back for more, so a positive user experience is key.

Wholesalers are not limited to these items, so be bold and ask them if there are other services they can provide that other distillers have found useful, and which may be useful to you.

Like every option out there, there are a few downsides to wholesale services. Here are some risks to manage:

- Sparse marketing – with a vast product range at their disposal and competing customer priorities, marketing is not a wholesaler's strength, especially when delivery measures – fulfilment, delivered in full on time – are among the key performance indicators for all distribution business success.

- It's not all about you. The fact that you have successfully partnered with a wholesaler does not make you special. There are thousands of lines that need their love and attention, and your offering is just one. Their job is to move your goods. Your job is to compel customers to buy your goods.

- Limited reach – few wholesalers claim to have national distribution, particularly in large geographies such as Australia, Europe and the United States. That said, it may be a non-issue if your sales strategy targets specific regions that your wholesale partners can service day in, day out as a matter of course.

Some wholesalers offer a consolidation service and can prepare mixed shipments for customers: an attractive offering that does away with minimum order quantities and may be better value than doing it yourself. Think also about why a wholesaler is particularly strong at servicing a region. This region may be an opportunity for your business to consider, even if it was not originally top of mind.

What is a distributor?

Wholesalers and distributors are interchangeable from a functional viewpoint. It would be reasonable to think that they are one and the same thing if you solely considered business functions, but from an operational viewpoint, there are differences which may influence your decision making so that it is consistent with your business plan and distribution strategy:

- Portfolios – wholesalers ship a raft of products as varied as rice, beer, grocery items, snacks, wine, bread and spirits. Distributors hone their portfolios to specific product types and categories.

- Marketing support – this is a significant service difference and advantage for distributor partnerships.

- Industry insights – specialist distributors can offer customer insights due to the niched nature of the product offerings.

- International brands – distributors will often stock well-known sought-after international brands, with good reason. They are financially strong, experienced in the industry and have resources available to support sales and marketing activities. Established brands and businesses are easy to work with.

- Niche customers – some distributors focus on the hospitality trade, such as restaurants and bars. This plays nicely into the super-premium plus product category that craft spirits belong to.

- Distributors may have sales representatives with incentives based upon product pull-through. This type of arrangement can provide motives for brand focus.

However, here is a cautionary note if you're considering approaching a distributor as one of your first steps toward world domination in craft spirits. Again, it's not all about you. There are easier ways for a distributor to make money than holding a new operation's hand.

How to be a great business partner

Take an interest in the industry beyond your operational facility. Talk to seasoned campaigners who can help you to navigate some of the traps that novices may fall into. Novices in this case can include people with distribution experience who have not dealt with craft spirits before. Sure, in principle it is a fast-moving consumer good that requires shifting from A to B, but there are a few specific nuances associated with moving craft spirits.

For example, how do you treat damaged freight when each item commands a value anywhere between $75 and $300? How do you manage product recalls from the field? What implications are there for excise and record keeping if the returned stock is unsalvageable, or indeed sustains damage upon return? What implications are there for the producer?

Investing time with experienced people will help set you up for long-term success, expand your network of relationships through trust and nurture your reputation as being a delight to work with. Focus on your business and your partners' business with transparency, teamwork and customer service; the rest will look after itself. Don't be an 'askhole': someone who seeks advice, and then does the opposite or completely ignores the advice. That is a sure-fire way to ensure that your favourite fan will not only need cleaning but replacing.

PRO TIP

Recognise, understand and master your role when it comes to being a great business partner in one of the most exciting industries in the world.

The product value journey

Once have a good handle on your COGS, you can make an accurate assessment of how much it will cost to make a bottle of your elixir. While you are on the DIY distribution route, you're taking the full margin that direct sales attract – but what about when you get others on board?

> ### EXERCISE: Your planning model
>
> Here's a rough planning model to consider if you choose to involve services from third parties to support your sales strategy. I'm using a super-premium plus product and the three channels discussed as the basis for this exercise:
>
> - DIY
> - Distributor
> - Wholesaler
>
> Assumptions:
>
> - Super-premium plus brands command retail prices excluding taxes that reflect provenance, high quality, care and attention.
> - Distributors demand a 25% margin to make it worth their while to partner with you.
>
> Estimate that wholesalers need 12% margin as their services are not as extensive as dedicated distributors delivering niche products.

For illustration, consider your base price as $AU45.

Channel	Percentage	Selling price to the channel	Margin
Direct	100%	$65	$20
Wholesaler	12%	$50.40	$14.60
Distributor	25%	$ 56.25	$11.25

This rather sobering table illustrates that if you sell direct to a customer for $65, taking the full $20 margin per bottle, this quickly erodes when you need help to scale up with third parties. Your margin reduces by $5 per bottle wholesale and $10 from a distributor. This trades off against the additional sales through supply by third parties and your ability to reach more customers than you could physically supply on your own.

Your options in this case are to:

- Set a higher retail price at the start; market conditions can help determine what this will be. Overseas and local brands will influence your price and positioning.

- Reduce your manufacturing overheads and material costs.

- Negotiate and agree margins with the wholesale and distribution businesses that work well for both parties.

- Include the shipping cost in pricing negotiations. Most consumers expect this to be included in the bottle price.

There is more to a distribution strategy than merely getting a distributor or wholesaler on board. It is about planning every element of how you get your product to market. The differences lie in scale, geographic range and the levels of customer service you intend to meet.

A distribution strategy needs to consider the specific means to supply your customers that balance reach, cost and customer service in ways that benefit the producer and the distributor.

Distribution trends

eCommerce is the trend of today. In ten key markets, including Australia, the IWSR forecast that the value of eCommerce trade would exceed $US42 billion in 2024, up from $US17 billion in 2019.[137] This presents a great opportunity for producers and distribution services in those markets,[138] meaning you need investment in technology and to optimise connectivity options that ISPs can provide for your business.

It also means answering a few questions, such as which delivery companies will you use? What shipping rates will you charge your customers? Free shipping creates ease for the customer and is great for marketing, or you may consider flat rates, tiered rates or real-time shipping rates via plugins or widgets. What packaging will you use to send the orders? Done well, this means packages arrive safely, so you could consider it as part of your branding and marketing strategy.[139]

Before the lockdowns and venue closures of the COVID-19 pandemic, the most profitable channel for craft spirits producers was on-premises trade: people who go out to drink. When this channel was no longer in play, their attention had to turn to innovative product offerings and means of supply. Online shopping became the channel of the day, driven mainly by existing consumer behaviour with fast-moving goods, and the confidence people had in the systems and infrastructure to deliver what they wanted when they needed it. Craft spirits makers had a lifeline, a way to maintain connection with their consumers that was both familiar and reassuring.

People invest lots of time and effort into online shopping, though not necessarily with the sole purpose to order alcohol. Often, supermarkets are in position to supply alcoholic products, as are off-licences and bottle stores. What this means is that a channel that craft spirits makers probably paid scant attention to in the past has come into focus. The place where this business transaction landscape will become bigger than Texas is in The Land of the Free.

CASE STUDY – THE RISE OF ECOMMERCE IN THE UNITED STATES[140]

The general view is that United States eCommerce has always been suspiciously subdued, caused in the main by the country's three-tier system of distribution restrictions. These constrain interstate business and complicate supply measures.

Craft spirits producers came up with innovative eCommerce approaches that used the three-tier system's shortcomings to their advantage. With new platforms emerging in the eCommerce space, people who never really understood that this type of supply solution was available came on board. With greater adoption came greater growth in a channel – dominated by China – that is the fastest-moving market in the world.

This table summarises the percentage of alcohol sales via eCommerce for China and the United States for 2019 and 2020:[141]

% sales from eCommerce	2019	2020
China	19%	10%
United States	19%	44%

Despite China being the global eCommerce market leader overall,[142] based on current growth trends, expectations are at the time of writing that the United States will overtake China in 2021. This is set against the backdrop of a trade war between the two nations.[143]

This happens to be good news for Australia's craft spirits makers, too. There is an opportunity for producers to figure out how to get their produce into the United States, particularly as 700 ml (70 cl) format is no longer a barrier to United States importation. If the cost constraints – attributable to the third highest excise tax rate in the world – on Australian spirit exports are eased, an exciting future awaits both countries.

CASE STUDY – THE UNITED STATES THREE-TIER SYSTEM OF ALCOHOL DISTRIBUTION

The current United States system arose following the repeal of prohibition in 1933.[144] The three tiers are:

- Tier 1 – importers (beer, wine or spirts makers) who may only sell their wares to wholesale distributors
- Tier 2 – distributors who may only sell to retailers
- Tier 3 – retailers who may only sell to consumers

The intent of the three-tier system was to prohibit tied houses – on-premises outlets that must purchase some specific products for sale – and to prevent 'disorderly marketing conditions'.

There are a few exceptions: brewpubs can be considered a producer and retailer without the need for a distributor. This can open the door to craft spirits makers as well. Then there are the seventeen states – referred to as Alcohol Beverage Control states – whose governments maintain a Tier 2 monopoly for distilled spirits.[145] They can still be referred to as having three tiers, albeit one tier is the government and not a private enterprise. Legislatures in Utah and Pennsylvania maintain Tier 2 and Tier 3 monopolies.

A bitter-sweet example is the state of Washington where the three-tier system was dismantled in 2011, replaced by a private retail route to market that now has the dubious honour of carrying the most heavily taxed spirits in the country. At 50% the rate in Washington, Oregon sports the second highest rate in the country.

Wherever you happen to be in the world, this case study demonstrates the wisdom in researching the channels to consider within your overall distribution strategy. It's amazing to see how creative and imaginative thinkers have embraced eCommerce as a means to address the disadvantages in the three-tier system. There may be something similar in your part of the world to consider, too.

CASE STUDY – COVID-19 IMPACT UPON SUPPLY

Meeting demand in an evolving trading landscape presented challenges to craft spirits makers and their supply chains during the COVID-19 pandemic. International air travel was curtailed in a fashion without precedent. This had a dramatically adverse effect upon duty-free sales, the segment known as global travel retail. IWSR analysis and research indicated that this sales channel would struggle to regain relevance until 2024.[146]

Because of the flexible working arrangements and absence from offices introduced by the pandemic and the resultant lockdowns, anecdotal evidence suggested that alcohol consumption per capita increased. Evidence in Australia drew a different conclusion, despite innovative ways to supply house-bound consumers and the rise of 'Zoom Drinks'. In a study conducted by the Australian National University,[147] 53% of Australians reported their alcohol consumption remained unchanged, and a further 27% reported their alcohol consumption decreased. The total sales of alcoholic beverages were significantly impacted by COVID-19 restrictions from March to May 2020, with spirits manufacturers reporting volume declines of 21% for full-bottled spirits and a further 37% volume decline for RTDs.

Distribution risks to manage

Work out your breakeven quantities for each channel in turn – DIY, distributor and wholesaler – noting that the most profitable, at least in the first instance, is a cellar door or online channel. I have already covered a few of the risks to the distribution channel or channels you choose. Simple price modelling in an Excel spreadsheet can assist with the key calculations for breakeven quantities at different margins for a given range of channel discounts. You can then use these to determine your product's floor pricing and margin range in negotiation with specialist distributors who are willing to help.

Safety considerations

Someone, somewhere will be handling your stock. Maybe it is you. Or it may be others. In either case, the goods must be safely packaged, without leaks and in good condition for shipment. This premise applies to all goods leaving your facility in response to any order from any channel.

Proof of delivery is a vital document to keep on hand in case there are queries about deliveries or disputes with customers concerning late payments. If people are taking stock for delivery from your facility, make sure that they are licenced to do so, and that the vehicle they use is registered, insured and fit for purpose. Make sure that whoever is collecting the goods is who you're expecting to do so. It can be easy to lose track of who is doing what when operations get busy.

Ensure that all invoice and shipment details align. Simple things like incorrect address details can be a nightmare to resolve after despatch, so take the time to get the little things right.

There are technology concerns as well. Make sure that your information technology systems are kept up to date with patches, antivirus, passphrases (passwords are now easier to break than ever before) and two-factor authentication. Use hardware and software applications that are fit for purpose, secure and with redundancy in place. Your personal and business data security is paramount for all transactions, especially those of a financial nature. Do not share passphrases or passwords and ensure that you change them regularly.

Summary

- What channels will you use for distribution: DIY, wholesaler or distributors? Consider the pricing impacts of each one.

- Look at the opportunities presented to you by the rise of eCommerce.

- What shipping rates will you use for your customers?

- Work out your breakeven quantities for each channel in turn – DIY, distributor and wholesaler.

- It is essential to ensure that all products leaving your facility are packaged safely.

- Don't underestimate the importance of the proof of delivery document.

- Check that the person collecting goods from your facility is licenced and is exactly who you are expecting.

- Never share passwords or phrases. Personal and business data protection is paramount.

Conclusion

That, my friends, is how we do it. The craft spirits business is a hero's journey: an epic call to adventure that many have undertaken and returned victorious and transformed. This applies equally to missionaries, mercenaries and misfits.

If you feel that starting a distillery is the right thing for you to do right now, then this book will guide you. In Part One, we explored what the crafts spirits industry is and why now is a great time to join it. We looked at the SPIRIT process, a framework designed to explore and understand the various considerations when you scope, plan, integrate, review and implement your vision, all in preparation for your time to shine in the marketplace, setting it against the cash drivers – product, brand/marketing and distribution – and creating the basis for a draft business plan. This will identify gaps and areas that expert help can address.

Part Two looked at the business plan in detail, then in Part Three, we became better acquainted with the cash drivers. Planning to run a successful business with a great team to bring your vision to life is hard. Running a business by yourself without a business plan is nigh on impossible. Which will you choose?

No *Gin Ventures* narrative would be complete without a challenge. After all, this is merely a new beginning, the start of an adventure into a world that sometimes seems supernatural. Magical, even. Here is my challenge to you; it's simple, but not easy:

Plan for bigger.

Think beyond what you have in mind today. Think about your legacy. Think about your sense of guardianship. Think about the future, and shape that future based upon your own narrative, background and sense of place.

The pursuit of a distillery business may drive interest in complementary businesses, linked to your sense of purpose and consistent with the business plan: a bar; a restaurant; accommodation; a tourist centre. Not everyone takes on the challenge when they hear the clarion call to adventure, but you are different – you are exceptional.

Be bold. Enjoy yourself. Apply the SPIRIT process in the spirit it's intended and create your own narrative. A remarkable future awaits.

Additional Resources

This list is not exhaustive – there is only so much one can place in a book. Here are my top educational resources to investigate, in addition to those covered off on your *Gin Ventures* journey.

Distillery business courses

Scotland – Heriot-Watt University, Master of Science in Brewing and Distilling: This program prepares candidates for entry into the malting, brewing or distilling industries, or to conduct research. It covers a broad range of subjects, from brewing science and chemical engineering to business studies and production management. Find out more at www.hw.ac.uk/ documents/pams/202122/B947-BRD_202122.pdf

United Kingdom – Practical Commercial Distilling Course, the Artisan Distiller, Jamie Baxter: This combines the five-day Practical Commercial Distilling Course with an additional one-day Advanced Gin Course and a gin tasting masterclass. For more information, head to www.brew-school.com/courses/practical-commercial-distilling-course-and-gin-masterclass-(6-days)-june

Australia – The Distillers Institute, Planning Your Successful Distilling Business: This course takes you on a targeted journey, covering everything you need to know to plan your own distillery, from thinking through ideas, to finances and working out all the things to purchase along the way. Consider this course – more details at www.thedistillersinstitute.com/store – as the starting point for thinking about a distillery business.

Product knowledge courses for business planning

Global – General Certificate in Distilling, Institute of Brewing and Distilling (IBD): IBD qualifications are the most widely recognised distilling qualifications in the world. The General Certificate in Distilling (www.ibd.org.uk/ibd-qualifications/distilling-qualifications/general-certificate-in-distilling) demonstrates that you understand the basic scientific principles of the distillation process that underpin producing a quality product.

Global – Wine and Spirit Education Trust (WSET):
The WSET is the largest global provider of wine, spirits and sake qualifications. Trusted by drinks organisations everywhere, WSET has led the design and delivery of wine and spirit education for five decades. With four progressive levels of study offered through course providers in more than seventy countries and translated into multiple languages, WSET inspires and empowers drinks professionals and enthusiasts. Find out more at www.wsetglobal.com/qualifications/?subject=Spirits

United States – Gin Course, Dr Gary Spedding, founder Brewing and Distilling Educational Services (BDES), Lexington, Kentucky: BDES invites the leading experts in the field of distilled spirits production to teach in dedicated classrooms. You will receive a quality education with lots of one-to-one attention and group discussions. For more details, head to https://bdastesting.com/app/uploads/2021/01/bdesgincourse2021_01_05.pdf

Licencing requirements

For licencing requirements in Australia, head to www.ato.gov.au/Forms/Licence-to-manufacture-alcohol

For licencing requirements in Aotearoa/New Zealand, visit www.customs.govt.nz/business/excise/apply-for-a-licence

Notes

1 From the foreword to M Thompson, *Still Magic: A gin distiller's guide for beginners* (Rethink Press, 2019)
2 https://pod.co/still-magic/molly-troupe-freeland-spirits
3 https://time.com/4357493/muhammad-ali-dead-best-quotes
4 www.businessinsider.com.au/johnnie-walkers-owner-just-bought-into-an-australian-whisky-distillery-2015-12
5 www.barrons.com/articles/a-global-ginnaissance-1513659181
6 www.chasedistillery.co.uk
7 https://sipsmith.com/our-story/our-team
8 https://sacredgin.com/pages/origin
9 https://castleandkey.com
10 www.youtube.com/watch?v=mHgcGH_3h6c&feature=youtu.be
11 www.afr.com/life-and-luxury/food-and-wine/at-lark-the-whisky-sets-the-agenda-even-if-the-timing-s-awkward-20210120-p56vkz
12 https://pod.co/still-magic/gavin-hughes-karen-touchie-stony-creek-farm
13 www.theiwsr.com/craft-gains-ground-in-australian-drinks-market

14 www.youtube.com/watch?v=fMOlfsR7SMQ
15 www.usmagazine.com/celebrity-news/news/
    muhammad-ali-dead-at-74-10-of-his-greatest-
    quotes-w208811
16 www.youtube.com/watch?v=REWeBzGuzCc
17 www.hhhdistill.com
18 www.burnswelding.com.au; www.theaislingdistillery.com.
    au
19 www.stillsmiths.com.au
20 https://pod.co/still-magic/the-distillers-voice-broken-
    heart-spirits-part-2
21 https://pod.co/still-magic/molly-troupe-freeland-spirits
22 www.pozible.com
23 https://pod.co/still-magic/tom-anderson-pinckney-bend-
    distillery-part-1
24 http://australiandistillers.org.au/about-us
25 https://distilledspiritsaotearoa.org.nz
26 https://americancraftspirits.org
27 www.britishdistillersalliance.com
28 www.abc.net.au/news/2021-02-10/tas-man-burned-in-
    distillery-fire-identified-as-well-known-golf/13139508
29 www.bbc.co.uk/news/mobile/uk-england-
    lincolnshire-14188297
30 www.saiglobal.com/PDFTemp/Previews/OSH/as/
    as1000/1900/1940-2004(+A2).pdf
31 www.beca.com
32 www.allenhpe.co.uk
33 www.nfpa.org/News-and-Research/Publications-and-
    media/NFPA-Journal/2018/March-April-2018/Features/
    Safe-Distilling
34 www.theiwsr.com/beverage-alcohol-ecommerce-value-
    grows-by-42-in-2020-to-reach-us24-billion
35 www.theiwsr.com/beverage-alcohol-ecommerce-value-
    grows-by-42-in-2020-to-reach-us24-billion
36 www.linkedin.com/posts/four-pillars-gin_fourpillarsgin-
    activity-6804906187830784000-fIWv
37 https://pod.co/still-magic
38 www.scottishfield.co.uk/food-and-drink-2/whisky/
    australian-godfather
39 https://pod.co/still-magic/jamie-baxter-the-artisan-
    distiller
40 https://pod.co/still-magic/ally-ayres-nick-ayres-karu-
    distillery

41 https://capebyrondistillery.com
42 https://pod.co/still-magic/gavin-hughes-karen-touchie-stony-creek-farm
43 www.iwsc.net/news/spirits/worldwide-gin-producer-of-the-year-2020-four-pillars-distillery
44 M Thompson, Still Magic: A gin distiller's guide for beginners (Rethink Press, 2019), pp81–91
45 In Australia, this is 10 g of pure alcohol: www.health.gov.au/health-topics/alcohol/about-alcohol/standard-drinks-guide
46 https://herbusiness.com/blog/5-key-ingredients-successful-brand
47 www.zdnet.com/article/a-2-minute-history-of-us-industrial-design
48 www.pmi.org/pmbok-guide-standards/foundational/pmbok
49 www.ukessays.com/essays/hospitality/effects-of-the-lockout-laws-on-society-and-the-hospitality-industry.php
50 www.rand.org/news/press/2020/09/29.html
51 www.business.com/articles/triple-bottom-line-defined
52 www.iecex.com
53 https://pod.co/still-magic/jamie-baxter-the-artisan-distiller
54 https://pod.co/still-magic/ep-40-cameron-mackenzie-four-pillars
55 http://brewing-distilling.com/page2/ccarl-stills.html
56 www.stillsmiths.com.au
57 https://g-still.com/products/genio-still
58 https://vendomecopper.com/products/distillation-equipment
59 www.hhhdistill.com
60 www.burnswelding.com.au
61 www.stillsmiths.com.au
62 www.anton-paar.com/uk-en/products/group/density-meter
63 www.legislation.gov.au/Details/C2021C00274/Download
64 www.cityoflondondistillery.com
65 https://pod.co/still-magic/jamie-baxter-the-artisan-distiller
66 www.craftypint.com/brewery/218/six-string-brewing
67 www.ato.gov.au/Forms/Licence-to-manufacture-alcohol
68 www.ato.gov.au/uploadedFiles/Content/ITX/downloads/BUS18495n71905.pdf
69 www.ato.gov.au/Business/Excise-on-alcohol/Excise-licences-for-excisable-alcohol/Types-of-excise-licences—alcohol

70 www.ato.gov.au/business/excise-on-alcohol/alcohol-excise-terms/?anchor=Underbond#Underbond

71 www.customs.govt.nz/library/legislation/default.asp

72 www.alcohol.org.nz/management-laws/nz-alcohol-laws/sale-and-supply-of-alcohol-act-2012

73 https://treasury.gov.au/sites/default/files/2021-05/171663_australian_distillers_association_and_spirits_and_cocktails_australia.pdf, p5

74 https://treasury.gov.au/sites/default/files/2021-05/171663_australian_distillers_association_and_spirits_and_cocktails_australia.pdf, p33

75 www.ascm.org/learning-development/certifications-credentials/dictionary

76 www.subway.com/en-nz

77 G Wickman, *Traction: Get a grip on your business* (BenBella Books, 2012), Chapter 4

78 https://pod.co/still-magic/ep-40-cameron-mackenzie-four-pillars

79 www.timdwyer.net.au/podcast

80 www.mccc.edu/~lyncha/documents/stagesofcompetence.pdf

81 www.heapsgoodgin.com.au

82 https://pod.co/still-magic/marcelle-macewan-and-greg-noonan-sa-distilling-co

83 R Kiyosaki, *Rich Dad, Poor Dad: What the rich teach their kids about money*, 2nd edition (Plata Publishing, 2017)

84 https://junogin.com/story

85 www.forbes.com/sites/avidan/2012/07/05/when-it-come-to-bourbon-america-knows-jack/?sh=6e87591a7b8b

86 https://pod.co/still-magic/stuart-mackenzie-little-juniper

87 https://littlejuniperdistilling.com.au

88 www.youtube.com/watch?v=Xc4grW9x1Tg

89 www.afr.com/companies/luring-young-drinkers-is-only-half-the-battle-19980420-kb3wx

90 www.afr.com/companies/two-dogs-that-aint-no-lemons-19950213-kawdf

91 https://andyiles.com/portfolio/xlr8-alcoholic-cola

92 https://drink-mc.co.nz/pages/pals

93 https://basicbabe.co

94 https://whiskycast.com/u-s-to-allow-700ml-whisky-bottles-for-first-time

95 www.theiwsr.com/5-key-trends-that-will-shape-the-global-beverage-alcohol-market-in-2021

96 www.theiwsr.com/5-key-trends-that-will-shape-the-global-beverage-alcohol-market-in-2021
97 www.suggestgin.co.nz
98 www.theiwsr.com/5-key-trends-that-will-shape-the-global-beverage-alcohol-market-in-2021
99 https://drinksdigest.com/2021/05/12/sales-boom-new-look-udl/
100 www.insider.com/the-best-and-worst-burgers-at-mcdonalds-ranked-2019-11
101 www.youtube.com/watch?v=MKJjLwMUPJI
102 https://wealthygorilla.com/top-20-richest-rappers-world
103 www.nateliason.com/notes/lessons-22-immutable-laws-marketing-al-ries
104 www.bbc.co.uk/iplayer/episodes/b0071b63/the-apprentice
105 S Pieroux, *Let's Get Visible! Get brand clarity, stand out in your industry and supercharge your business growth* (Rethink Press, 2019)
106 Figure used with kind permission of Sapna Pieroux
107 www.indy100.com/people/remembering-when-muhammad-ali-invented-the-shortest-poem-in-the-english-language-7298996
108 www.greenallsgin.com/discover/the-history-of-greenalls/
109 https://pabstblueribbon.com
110 www.smirnoff.com/en-row
111 www.dogfish.com/front
112 www.bacardilimited.com
113 www.jimbeam.com/en-au
114 https://dosequis.com
115 www.barsclubs.com.au/bars-clubs/howlin-wolfs-boss-babe-bar-takeover
116 https://pod.co/still-magic/ally-ayres-nick-ayres-karu-distillery
117 https://vimeo.com/253715331
118 https://thestrategystory.com/2021/03/23/southwest-airlines-strategy
119 S Pieroux, *Let's Get Visible! Get brand clarity, stand out in your industry and supercharge your business growth* (Rethink Press, 2019)
120 www.abac.org.au/about/thecode
121 www.portmangroup.org.uk
122 www.ttb.gov/advertising/alcohol-beverage-advertising

123 https://colangelopr.com/2019/05/spirits-boom-why-craft-matters-to-millennials
124 www.upwork.com
125 www.fiverr.com
126 www.strangerandstranger.com
127 www.thespiritsbusiness.com/2016/01/millennial-consumers-shun-mass-market-spirits
128 https://youtu.be/e6E4e_noMpE
129 https://campaignbrief.com/johnnie-walker-launches-first
130 www.referralcandy.com/blog/johnnie-walker-marketing-strategy
131 https://cannybites.co.uk/portfolio-item/if-you-are-green-you-grow-2-2-5-2-21
132 https://heidicohen.com/marketing-the-4-moments-of-truth-chart
133 www.merchantscx.com/news/understanding-moments-of-truth-and-how-they-connect-to-customer-journeys
134 www.facebook.com/groups/cskool
135 www.abac.org.au/about
136 www.agw.org.au/assets/ABAC/ABAC-Best-Practice-in-Digital-Marketing-2016.pdf
137 www.youtube.com/watch?v=Xc4grW9x1Tg
138 Key markets are Australia, Brazil, China, France, Germany, Italy, Japan, Spain, USA, UK
139 www.business.gov.au/marketing
140 www.theiwsr.com/new-technology-drives-ecommerce-innovation-in-the-us
141 www.theiwsr.com/wp-content/uploads/IWSR-Press-Release_IWSR-Ecommerce-Study-China-leads-the-way-for-beverage-alcohol-ecommerce_5Sep2018.pdf
142 https://info.theiwsr.com/1/330251/2021-02-03/36ffnz
143 www.bbc.com/news/business-45899310
144 www.nabca.org/three-tier-system-modern-view-0
145 www.nabca.org/three-tier-system-modern-view-0
146 www.theiwsr.com/will-covid-19-disrupt-premiumisation-trends-in-the-global-travel-retail-channel
147 www.aihw.gov.au/reports/alcohol/alcohol-tobacco-other-drugs-australia/contents/impact-of-covid-19-on-alcohol-and-other-drug-use
148 www.ascm.org/learning-development/certifications-credentials/dictionary

Acknowledgements

Writing a book, like starting a business, raises a crucial question: who can help?

Bringing to life this latest book in the *Still Magic* series is no exception. I owe my thanks to the following people.

Bill Lark, your boundless energy, generosity and self-less contributions will ensure that the Australian craft spirits industry moves from strength to strength for decades to come. Rest assured: your legacy is in good hands. A bright future beckons thanks to the example you've set and leadership you've shown; better people make better distillers.

Releasing a manuscript for beta review is akin to standing naked on a weighing machine with a credit card statement strategically covering one's nether regions. The sense of vulnerability is real and discomfiting, despite the fact that, in this case, it is déjà vu.

A huge thank you to my beta-reader team: Holly Klintworth, Ross Hastings, Astral Sligo, Stewart Marshall and Amy Odongo for your patience and perseverance. It is a task that would drive most to drink and likely convince most distillers to consider teetotalism.

To my distilling family whom I mention in this book: from the bottom of my gin-filled heart, I thank you all.

When the thoughts of a *Still Magic* reprise became irresistible, I immediately knew who could help: the superb team at Rethink Press. There is no magic to unleash without my writing mentors Lucy McCarraher (the Upholder), Joe Gregory (the Rebel), Kathleen Steeden (Project Editor), Alison Jack (Copy Editor) and Anke Ueberberg (Publishing Manager). Thank you all for your support and guidance. Gin and tonics, shaken Martinis and French 75s all round.

Thank you, Lauren Orrell, for your superb camera work yet again.

My family have been supportive of my efforts for many years, and for that I am grateful.

Mary Thompson's sense of practicality was on point yet again. Mary helped me find creative ways to manage the 10pm Zoom calls, my need to read new paragraphs aloud, and consequently tending to a gin collection under threat from non-consumption. Thank you, my love. Ernest Hemingway would have been most pleased.

Julia Vale Gamble, thank you for delivering more design and creative wizardry. Your work moves from strength to strength, bringing life and texture to the *Gin Ventures* narrative.

Thanks also to my brother Pita Thompson. A successful coach in rugby union, touch rugby and basketball, he is also a dual-national-level representative in two sports. He has been an understated influence throughout my spirits journey. His example has shown me that time spent nurturing inexperience successfully removes barriers to success. Legacies begin when skills are developing – and exciting futures await those with vision.

Kia manawa kai tūtae – be bold

Kia ngahau ai – enjoy yourself

Kia waihangatia tō ake pūrākau – create your narrative

The Author

Marcel Thompson (*Ngāti Whātua, Waikato, Ngāti Koata*) is an award-winning gin maker whose career began as an assistant distiller in New Zealand in the 1980s. He is a podcast host and the author of Amazon bestseller *Still Magic: A gin distiller's guide for beginners* (Rethink Press, 2019).

His experience spans both traditional and contemporary distilling operations. His unique skillset has seen him facilitate joint ventures with international and domestic partners, and to commercialise new product concepts for craft distilleries. He is an advocate for the Australasian craft spirits industries and their practitioners.

Marcel is passionate about safety, education, high-quality product delivery and commercial problem solving.

🌐 www.stillmagic.net

🎙 https://pod.co/still-magic

▪ www.facebook.com/marcelstillmagic

🐦 Marcel@Still_Magic

📷 @stillmagicway

🔗 www.linkedin.com/in/marcel-thompson-62baa01

Ingram Content Group UK Ltd.
Milton Keynes UK
UKHW020919290623
424249UK00014B/445